On Divorce Row

Redemption~Recovery~Restoration

Leonie Leo-Brewer

EVANGELISTA MEDIA™ srl
Via Maiella, 1
66020 San Giovanni Teatino (Ch) – Italy

"Changing the World, One Book at a Time"

This book and all other Evangelista Media™ and Destiny Image™ Europe books are available at Christian bookstores and distributors worldwide.

To order products, or for any other correspondence:
EVANGELISTA MEDIA™ srl
Via Maiella, 1
66020 San Giovanni Teatino (Ch) – Italy
Tel. +39 085 959806 • Fax: +39 085 9090113
Email: info@evangelistamedia.com
Or reach us on the Internet: www.evangelistamedia.com

ISBN: 978-88-6880-115-1
ISBN eBook: 978-88-6880-116-8

For Worldwide Distribution, Printed in Italy.
1 2 3 4 5 6 / 21 20 19 18

Acknowledgments

There are several people I would like to thank for supporting me in making this book a reality. First and foremost, I thank my Abba Father, my Lord Jesus Christ and Holy Spirit with all my heart and soul for giving me life. His love and grace covered my multitude of sins, which helped me to forget my old life and walk in my new life as a daughter of the Most High God, which is who He created me to be. His lifeblood cleansed me and gave me the power and authority to walk in my calling, as a powerful woman of God. I thank Him for giving me the gift of writing, which I dedicate to serving Him and the church until I see Him face-to-face one day.

My thanks and appreciation must start with my parents. They taught my siblings and me who God was and that we had to worship and devote ourselves to Him and the church. They also showed us what marriage and family looked like practically by staying together for 63 years of marriage! I am so grateful that I had the opportunity to tell my mom what an impact she had made on my life before she passed away in February 2016. Thank you to the best parents in the world!

To my husband, Kevin: Love, without your love and support with every step I've taken on this journey of finding my true identity in Christ, I would not be the woman I am today. I am so proud to be your wife and so proud of how you have raised the bar in becoming a man after God's heart. I am so proud of how you have built your business and faced challenges head-on. The way we have weathered storms together is a testimony of God's grace in our marriage. Thank you, my Love, from the bottom of my heart. And a special thank you for all your support in looking after my beloved father after my precious mom passed away. I stand with you and declare: As for me and my house, we will serve the Lord!

A special thank you to my very precious daughters, Sherinne and Julie: "I'm so sorry," does not even come close to how sorry I am that you suffered the pain of my decision to divorce your father. Thank you for forgiving me and for loving me regardless. Your lives are a blessing to me. My commitment to you both and your husbands and families is to pray every day that God would bless you more than you have suffered, and that He will bring good out of the bad. Also I thank you, Bruce and Brent, for loving my daughters and grandchildren and making them your first priority. I'm so proud of you both and couldn't have asked for better sons-in-law.

I also acknowledge the positive impact of all my families, extended families, and the many friends who have walked this journey with us over the past twenty years. There are some friends who have walked with me since I was a young woman, like my dear friend Merle. I'm sorry I can't mention everyone by name, but you know who you are. Without your love and encouragement, Kevin and I would not be where we are today! Thank you one and all from both of us. What you have sown and invested in our lives, I pray will return to you one hundredfold and then some!

To my younger sister Bev: thank you for the gift of Andrew Jobling's *One Word at a Time* writing course, which gave me the push I needed to start writing this book.

Thank you to all our prayer partners, particularly Louise Steenkamp, one of my dearest friends, and Lizelle Pieterse who has spent more hours in prayer for my family and me than anyone else I know. Thank you all from the bottom of my heart for all the hours you spent praying for Kevin and me and our family over many years. There will be eternal rewards!

To Munya, Eddie, and staff at Imaginate Communications, you have done an excellent job with designing my website! Thank you so much for the very professional work. Thank you, Munya and Bertha, also for the spiritual impartation into my life, it has been spiritually rewarding for me.

To my publisher, Dr. Pietro and Sandra Evangelista and the excellent team at Evangelista Media, I thank you for being obedient to the call from our Father to publish first-time authors. I treasure our relationship and look forward to more books being published with your excellent publishing house!

To Tyronne and Stacey at Pinkyshade, I love my photos! You have created an extraordinary woman out of a very ordinary one with your gifted creativity! Thank you—you guys rock!

And last but not least, to our precious grandchildren: Megan Clare (13), Dylan Riley (10), Luke Mark and Jordan Reece (10): *On Divorce Row* is dedicated to the four of you. Right now, you are too young to read this book, or take note of the content, but my and Grandpa's prayer is that as you grow and learn the real truth of who you are in Christ, of how much Jesus loves you, you will carry that truth in your hearts throughout your lives. We pray that together with your spouses, you will love and serve the Lord all the days of your lives and consider that service to be a priority and a privilege. May divorce not enter your homes and may marriage be your highest calling. Whether we live to see the fruits of our prayers or not, know this, each one of you is extremely special and unique, and God has a wonderful plan for your life, if you will follow Him and stay on His path. Life without Him is pointless. We are the most blessed grandparents in the world, and we thank Father God for giving us the privilege of being your grandparents! We love you all to the moon and back!

Praises for *On Divorce Row*

When I opened Leonie's book, I was immediately captured by two irrefutable truths she had stated on the very first page: the first being that God redeems our story so that our past won't become someone else's future; and the other, is that just about every one of us has directly or indirectly been affected by divorce and I, not less than anyone else, with both my parent's double divorces.

I was immediately riveted and knew that I needed to hear her story so I too could learn from it. I recognized the hand of God and His soft voice speaking to me through her testimony. Sometimes laughing, sometimes crying, as I could associate with what she imparted. This book is certainly very applicable to every one of us—God's beautiful and blessed female creation, and it certainly won't hurt our male counterparts to read it too!

I found that this book had a message for us all and that it caters to all manners of learning. It includes facts and references for those who learn best from information and teachings, and it includes her real-life stories for those who learn best from other's examples. In her writing, Leonie has been open, honest, and transparent, as she shares her ideals, failures, disappointments, hardships, hopes, and victories. I know that as difficult as her journey has been, none of it has been in vain. Through the selfless sharing of her life's story with us, countless women (and men) can learn, receive hope, be encouraged, and experience victory.

We live in a world today that is hammering our brains with easy solutions—instant coffee, surfing the Web for quick answers and services, instant food and quick deliveries—everything to make life easier and cater to our every whim. In this day and age, to a greater or lesser degree, we have lost the art of waiting. To take the time and effort to make something; striving until we have reached our goal. For example, waiting for vegetables to grow and being content to wait for summer to give us cucumbers (as did our grandparents), working hard on relationships and persevering. We want everything and we want it yesterday!

With all the quick and easy solutions available today, we have forgotten that relationships take time and effort. They require self-sacrifice. They require praying, trusting the Lord, and waiting for breakthroughs. We have been conditioned to falsely believe that everything revolves around ME and MY happiness. We believe the fairy tale; thus, reality trips us up every time. We have forgotten that happiness is found in trying, serving, persevering, faithfulness, and attaining small victories. Instead, today, we so often enter into marriage with an exit sign, called DIVORCE, like a sign blinking brightly in the background on a door. I know I did, and it hasn't contributed to my marriage at all.

Instead, it has stolen from me and harmed my marriage relationship. It took God and His faithfulness for me to burn that door! The world offers divorce as a solution to hardship and not getting our own way, sending broken people more broken into the world to fend for themselves in a lonely, hostile environment. God offers real change, healing, and restoration and uniting two diverse people in a lovely God-way on His platform of love, peace, and unity, a platform that offers a friend and comrade to stand with you to face the world.

God's way offers a safe (albeit imperfect) haven in which children can grow up emotionally and spiritually healthy until they take their own place in the world and continue Jesus' legacy. However, what it takes is for us to bend our stubborn, self-serving necks and obey Him and remember that the best things in life are worth fighting for.

This brings me to one of the most profound truths found in *On Divorce Row*: marriage is not a contract between two parties—it is between three, God being the most important and faithful party. All through *On Divorce Row* we see clearly God's faithfulness to marriage. If only one of a couple determines to save the marriage, that one is not alone; in reality, God and that person are both fighting for the marriage.

Leonie's testimony is a God-testimony. Through everything—the ups and the downs, the good times and difficult times, the hopes and disappointments, whether they were strong or weak—we see how God has been there, how He has fought for them, how He has been faithful, how He has healed and answered prayers, how He has brought them victory. *On Divorce Row* is a life story of hope where we recognize that God will always be a partner to those who want to save their marriage.

On Divorce Row is not a fairy tale, but a realistic rendition of common challenges we all face in relationships. It calls readers to take stock of their own relationship and to challenge the status quo. By using her acquired knowledge and own experiences as examples, we can relate to, it helps readers confront difficulties and problems and deal with them God's way. Leonie's interesting and practical examples give depth to the advice and teaching shared in her book. She has learned valuable lessons in life and shares them in such a way as to make them practically applicable to others.

Leonie also addresses the emotional and spiritual affect her challenges and decisions have had on her and her family, which can help readers avoid making the same mistakes. Hers is a story of running to the Father and clinging to Him, hoping and deliberately putting her faith in Him and the promises in His Word, even when things looked impossible. Hers is a testimony of perseverance even when her knees buckled, which ultimately leads to victory! Hers is a testimony of hope!

I've had the privilege of knowing Leonie for almost two decades. Although we have often lived far apart, she has been one of my best friends all through these years, with whom I could share my woes, knowing she will not judge, but rather pray with me and for me and give sound advice. She has been an example to me as a woman who diligently studies the Word and pursues a relationship with Jesus. She has been a motivation to me on how to persevere and put my faith into action. I have always been amazed by how she would submit to God's way even when it was the last thing she wanted to do, and how she would keep trusting Him even though she didn't get a quick answer.

Since I've known Leonie, I've seen her appropriate God's will in all her relationships: with her husband, children, parents, friends, etc.

She diligently prays for them. She always seeks and pursues the best for them, even in the midst of raging hormones and heartaches. Leonie has a deep and loving heart, cares genuinely, and serves others selflessly. She is an avid student, and what she shares is knowledgeable, truthful, trustworthy, and tempered by experience. Leonie is truly as her name means: "lioness, one with a courageous spirit," with the Scripture reference Psalm 25:5 (NKJV), "Lead me in Your truth and teach me, for You are the God of my salvation; on You I wait all the day."

Thank you, Leonie, for being willing to share your life with us. You are indeed a golden vessel in God's hands!

Lizelle Pieterse
Missionary with CCC for 26 years
Leader of GAIN
(Global Aid Network, the humanitarian arm of CCC)
in South Africa

~

This book is full of wisdom and written in love and concern for all couples struggling in their relationships, pre-marriage, and in marriage, and especially those in danger of their marriages disintegrating.

This autobiography is full of warnings that emanate from Leonie's life story and will be of special help to the next generation, where she passionately implores young adults to make decisions that please God and are for their own well-being. These are specifically in terms of relationships with the opposite sex.

Leonie recounts her life in detail; and out of each era, she describes the tough times and shows her real walk with the Lord and battle to overcome, acknowledging her weaknesses and showing her increased dependence on God to help her in her marriage. Her longing to warn her readers of potential hazards is clearly evident as she describes issues that affect couples at various stages of their lives. This book simultaneously reveals the depth of Leonie's growth in her walk with the Lord, and His entrusting her with platforms to share godly wisdom. This is an exciting journey for readers to experience.

Leonie gives a deep, yet simple Bible study, relating to each stage of her life—from her early childhood to her present-day life. Every reader can reap pearls of wisdom throughout, accompanying her on her journey.

As we worked together as colleagues, Leonie shared many of her experiences with the Lord with me. As a ladies' ministry, we were blessed to hear her input at Apples of Gold (Titus 2 mentorship) retreats. We could see over those years, that the Lord had given her special writing ability and great insight into growing into women of God (we utilized several of her studies in our resources, which included a description of a woman of inner beauty and a woman of worth).

The success of journaling, as encouraged by Leonie, has influenced many lives of people who journal events and talk with the Lord as they do it, being aware of God's daily presence, and finding journaling to be life-changing and worthwhile. For this reason, I heartily recommend that readers journal as they go through the following chapters with the Lord. He may lead in a special way as you do this. Thank you, Leonie! Thank you, too, for fighting on for the cause of righteousness and for being so honest and real!

Bev van Rensburg
Student Counselor
South African Theological Seminary

Contents

Preface

A funny quote from *Top 40 Funny Divorce Quotes* says, "Marriage is one of the chief causes of divorce." I include this quote with tongue in cheek, but it does highlight the underlying point that unless we make the effort to get our marriages on track, God's way, we will more than likely end up being just another statistic in the divorce court. And statistics say that one divorce affects sixteen people. If you picked up this book to read, the chances are that you have either been directly or indirectly affected by divorce. Read on; *On Divorce Row* was written for you!

For homes to be free of divorce and filled with godly marriages and families (and in that way, create godly communities and nations), marriages and families must get back to the way God originally intended them to be. Jesus says in Matthew 19:8 that "Moses permitted divorce only as a concession to your hard hearts, but it was not what God had originally intended."

On Divorce Row was written so that families of every tongue, tribe, and nation will join God in building godly homes, restoring marriages and families, and eradicating divorce. Christians have to answer the question: "If not us, then who?"

The divorce rate in South Africa and around the world is at an all-time high. Some of the more common reasons being:

> Couples not willing to work on their marriages

> Couples not understanding God's original intention for marriage

> Couples not understanding the crippling effect of divorce on children and the family unit

> Husbands not taking up their rightful place as leaders, providers, and protectors of their families and homes

➤ Addiction to pornography, alcohol, infidelity, and substance abuse (to name a few)

➤ Couples choosing cohabitation over marriage

➤ Debt and financial struggles

➤ Parents abdicating their God-given mandate to train their children in the admonition of the Lord

➤ Men and women increasingly turning to homosexuality and lesbianism and raising adopted children in same-sex homes

➤ Lack of communication and conflict resolution skills

➤ Lack of understanding the fear of the Lord

On Divorce Row was written as a warning of the devastation that can happen through divorce. Preventative measures are included, particularly for people contemplating divorce, preparing for marriage, and in marital strife.

I have been divorced twice and married three times. I know what I am talking about when I say that divorce shatters lives of family members now and in generations to come. Everything that God created carries eternal rewards, and we need to consider what legacy we're leaving to our children—is it rewarding? Marriage is God's idea and cannot be taken lightly or carnally. If we live marriage God's way, we will reap eternal rewards now and, more importantly, leave a godly legacy to the generations that follow.

I wrote *On Divorce Row* because of the devastation divorce caused me and my family. To be honest, if I knew then what I know now, I don't believe divorce would have been an option.

Divorce is not the unforgivable sin. Neither is remarriage. But we can learn from experienced people, like myself, how to prevent the heartache and the pain of divorce and remarriage by understanding why God says "I hate divorce!" (Malachi 2:16).

At the same time, we learn about the Father's great and unending love for those who live with a sense of guilt and condemnation over their decision to divorce. Let God's grace and mercy wash away every trace of pain and hurt, as *On Divorce Row* reveals the real truth of God's amazing grace, available to those who choose to dedicate their lives and families to Him.

Chapter 1

The Birth of a Dream Life

We need to see each child as a gift, to be welcomed, cherished and protected. –Pope Francis

Sometimes God redeems your story by surrounding you with people who need to hear your past so it doesn't become their future. May my past never become your future!

I don't know anyone within the circle of my friends and families who have not, either directly or indirectly been touched by divorce. Having said that, the chances are if you have purchased this book you are probably *On Divorce Row* and need to hear my past so that it doesn't become your future.

Authors are encouraged to write with the end in mind, and that is what I have done. As you read this book, my prayer is that the Holy Spirit would challenge you to stop where you are right now. Take stock of your marriage. Reevaluate your marriage and family situation. Then ask yourself this question—maybe for the first time, but more likely for the umpteenth time—*Is divorce really the solution to our problems?* It's been my experience that divorce is seldom the solution to marital problems. Obviously there are exceptions, but God made a man and a woman to be one in marriage and that oneness is what is difficult, if not impossible, to dissolve.

On the other hand, only you can be the judge of your own actions. Does my book make for good comfortable reading? Good, definitely! Comfortable, unfortunately it does not. It wasn't written for comfort or relaxation. Rather, it was written to challenge the status quo that most married couples find themselves in today. In this sin-sick world. There is a saying here in Africa that goes like this: "Marriage is not for sissies!"

That saying means marriage takes time and effort, and only the strong, long-suffering, and steadfast make it to the end. So read on and be challenged to confront the hard things in your relationship and to deal with them God's way.

At the Beginning

In order to do the title *On Divorce Row* justice, I need to outline the foundation of my life, beginning at the beginning.

My parents were born in South Africa, as were my eldest brother and sister. My parents had never ventured outside of their hometown, Durban; that was until sometime around 1956 when a recession in South Africa caused my dad to assess his family's situation. That assessment turned his eyes toward a country called Rhodesia (now Zimbabwe) where the economy was booming at that time. I am not sure why my father chose Rhodesia, but he decided to leave South Africa to make Rhodesia, in particular, a town called Umtali (now Mutare), his family's new home.

My parents were raised in Durban and after they married they lived close to my maternal grandparents, my mother's siblings, her extended family, and her close friends. They had always lived with family and friends around them. I'm sure it was traumatic leaving their home (particularly for my mother) and relocating to a strange and unfamiliar country, especially with two small children in tow. No doubt, my father would have debated the pros and cons of relocating to another country with my mother before making the final decision. I often wonder how she must have felt and where her thoughts went during that long, dry, and lonely 1,400-kilometer (870-mile) journey to the place they would eventually call home.

What were her first impressions, as they arrived in that strange and wonderful place? How did my siblings behave on the journey, given that there were no such conveniences as bottled baby food and disposable nappies? My brother was a very active toddler (or so we've been told), and it could not have been easy traveling that long distance keeping two small children occupied for so many hours.

What were my father's thoughts of uprooting his family to venture into unknown territory? He must have had some misgivings about whether he would find work, or even if the decision he made was the right one. It was a huge step he had taken, which unbeknown to him would one day have a huge impact on his family, then and for generations to come.

As mentioned previously, my family arrived in Rhodesia sometime in 1956. They stayed in a motel until my father found a job (he was a builder) and a small house to rent. They were still settling in when my mother found out she was pregnant. It was a huge shock and the thought of aborting the pregnancy crossed her mind. She obviously felt quite desperate at the time, given her circumstances—two toddlers, living in a rented home in a new country, and my father had just started a new job. Not the best environment to embrace the news of a baby on the way. But her attempts to abort the pregnancy failed and nine months later, on the June 17, 1957, I was born.

Much has been written regarding exactly what a baby can hear, feel, and experience in the uterus. For example, on some level, what the pregnant mother feels emotionally is transferred directly to her unborn child. Because of this phenomenon, constant negative emotions can have a damaging effect on the baby while still in the womb. Many years after I was born, I found out (and I now know it was probably due to my mother's reaction to the news of her pregnancy), that I had huge rejection issues, which manifested in all sorts of dysfunctional ways in my teen and adult years.

My younger brother was also born in Mutare. When my brother and I were still toddlers, my parents relocated to Bulawayo where we were raised, schooled, and where my parents bought a house and settled down for the next approximately twenty-one years. During those years, my younger sister was born, making us five children in total. My parents met many friends as they began settling down in Bulawayo; some of them they met at the Catholic Church where they were members.

What little girl, under the right circumstances, doesn't love her daddy's attention and affection? I was no exception. My father was my hero, my proverbial knight in shining armor. I adored him.

Often people would make comments like, "You can see whose child you are," "The apple doesn't fall far from the tree," and the favorite saying in those days, "You're definitely not the postman's daughter!" My parents told me about a time when I was admitted to the hospital to have an abscess drained from my knee. I was 18 months old and apparently cried nonstop for my father to come and get me, waking up all the other children in the ward until the staff were desperate and phoned my dad. He walked into the ward, and I stopped crying instantly when I saw him. I was just so happy to see him. At last, everything would be fine because Daddy was there.

It was the custom in Rhodesia for children to start school at the age of five. People were also far more neighborly than what they are today. As a family, we had several friends, who were also our neighbors. One of my parent's friends had a son my same age. In the mornings, my dad would walk with me to their house and then my little boy friend would take my case, hold my hand, and walk me to school. Even at the tender age of five, I recognized that it made me feel loved, cared for, and cherished. Consequently, I believe it was at that time that my desire, my dream, was birthed and began to grow deep in my heart.

DEFINING MOMENTS

What was the desire? To one day be a beautiful virgin bride, loved and cherished by my husband. A mom and a full-time homemaker. It felt good. Like a fairy-tale kind of feeling. My husband would be a tall, dark, and handsome man, I dreamt. We would love one another and live happily ever after until death do us part. That was the first defining moment in my life.

I loved everything about kindergarten and I was a diligent pupil. I thrived in school and I was a happy little girl with a cheerful disposition. When I was in grade four, I took up dancing—ballet, modern, tap, and later acrobatics. I was a good dancer, and by the time I was twelve, I entered many dance shows. I also completed dancing exams through the International Dance Teacher's Association and the Royal Academy of Dancing. One of the examiners of the International Dance Teacher's

Association said, "With more experience this girl will go far." I simply loved dancing and would have gone on to become a dance teacher if I had focused more on dancing than dating! But more about that later.

I also enjoyed athletics and I was a good athlete. I performed my best in short distance races, long jump, and gymnastics. I also won the *Victrix Ludorum* in junior school. These stories that I share with you all happened in kindergarten and junior school. I really was passionate about school.

However, as I became what is known today as a "tween" (the age between a child and a teenager), I began to sense changes in my thoughts and feelings about myself. I was friendly with three girls in school. These girls were in the popular group and it was cool to be friends with them. Suddenly, out of the blue, one day I started feeling inferior to these friends of mine. Feelings like they were better than me. As I compared myself to them, guess what happened. That's right, I came up short every time. I felt I wasn't as attractive as they were, nor did I have a figure like they had. Although I was an above average pupil in junior school, I believed they were far more academic than I was.

I cannot say that it was anything they did or said; rather, it was I who distanced myself from them emotionally and physically, because of an inferiority complex I had. This tendency to compare myself in a negative way to my friends continued as I entered high school, and got progressively worse. Two of these girls had good relationships with their parents. As I observed their close relationship with their parents, I began to doubt the love of my parents, especially the love of my father. I dwelt on it so much that I eventually convinced myself that my father did not love me and that my mother wished that the attempted abortion had been successful!

On some level, I knew that was a lie, but I was young and ignorant as to how the mind worked. I would be lying if I told you that I had an unhappy childhood—I didn't. My parents were emotionally distant, but that wasn't intentional. What parent in those days knew anything about being "emotionally distant"? Nevertheless, something changed in me when I became a tween. I wasn't particularly close to my sisters at that time. My older sister had her own friends. My younger sister went to a different school. So, my girlfriends were more like sisters to me as I was growing up, which made their apparent distance from me really devastating.

To make matters worse, my girlfriends found new friends and I became a sort of "reserve" friend (a friend they could use if their new friends were not available). I was crushed and started rebelling. I got into the wrong crowd at school—mostly with boys I got into mischief with, which landed us in a lot of trouble. I often spent time in detention because of the childish pranks, but some of them were also dangerous. When I look back on those days, I cringe.

At the same time, I also started bunking (skipping) school (more times than I care to remember or tell you—so embarrassing!), and I intercepted letters from the headmaster about my absence from school. So my parents never found out that (a) I was in trouble at school, and (b) I was bunking. Of course, I eventually got busted when my dad got the mail before I did one day. Oh boy! That blew everything wide open. [Sigh.] Obviously, I was punished; I was grounded for a month. Needless to say, I never did that again!

REGRETS

There have been many times over the past forty years when I've thought about the careless, rebellious acts of my youth and the regrets over the things I wish I had never done. On the other hand, I also regretted things I didn't do, like taking my education seriously—that being one of my biggest regrets. Education is important, and I missed the chance to study and qualify academically in preparation for a career in my adult years. I am however, grateful to my mother who insisted that I at least earn a year's secretarial diploma at college. That qualification has stood me in good stead in every employment I've had.

Not too long ago, a colleague and I were discussing our qualifications. I meekly told him that I actually didn't have any qualifications. He looked at me straight in the eye and said, "Wow, Leonie, you are so intelligent. Can you imagine where you would be today if you had applied yourself?" What does someone say to a statement like that? My answer was, "You're right, but I know now that it is never too late to be all God has called me to be."

I'd like to leave you with this thought: neither my parents, my friends, my teachers, or my family were to blame for the change in me or those rebellious years. So what was to blame?

As I close this chapter, I recall a bumper sticker I once saw: "It's Never Too Late to Have a Happy Childhood!" What do you think? True or false?

Don't go away. Stay with me as we explore that question together.

"BUT GOD" CHAPTER 1

At the end of each chapter, you will find a "But God" summary that will hopefully help you understand that God is working in every (good or bad) situation for His purposes. If I had to put a Scripture verse to this chapter (and I'll be doing just that at the end of every chapter), it would be, and is Genesis 50:20 (GNT):

> *You plotted evil against me, but God turned it into good, in order to preserve the lives of many people who are alive today because of what happened."* (Please read the full story in Genesis chapters 37-50.)

Some people might not agree with what I'm about to say, but I believe satan targeted my life for destruction before I was even born. He knew if I lived I would make an impact for the Kingdom. And here's the good news for this chapter: "But God" turned my life and satan's intention around for the good. God's plan and purpose for my life has always been a good one. And try as he might, satan will never be able to thwart the plan of God for my life—or for yours. I conclude my summary with the following point of view.

The first defining moment in your child's life is one of the most important, for obvious reasons. Be aware of what goes on in your child's life at all times. Things that we take for granted can be defining moments for your child—and at the age of five, they are unable to discern that. I was an innocent five-year-old, but my dream was birthed at that age and I was blissfully unaware of it.

Your children's friends are also of utmost importance. Be aware of how their friends make them feel. For example, do their friends bring the best out of them, or the worst? Are they insecure around their friends, or confident and happy? Do they get into mischief, or are they open and childlike? Do they act their age?

Stop what you're doing right now and do a mental assessment of the last few times your child was on a play date or had a friend over to play at your house. Was it arranged beforehand? Did they play well together? Were there any conflicts or disagreements between them or their siblings? What about their friend's family and home life?

Is it a stable home? Are their values like yours, or are there things that you accept for the sake of the friendship even though they conflict with the values and morals in your own home and life?

What are the biggest influencers at the moment in your child's life? Television, social media, Internet, books, friends, school, other family, toys/games, extramural activities, parents?

Verses to Meditate on and Memorize from Chapter 1

➤ Proverbs 22:6 (NKJV): *Train up a child in the way he should go, and when he is old he will not depart from it.*

➤ Ephesians 6:4 (GNT): *Parents, do not treat your children in such a way as to make them angry. Instead, raise them with Christian discipline and instruction.*

Journal your thoughts:

_____
_____
_____
_____
_____
_____
_____

Journal your prayer:

_____
_____
_____
_____
_____
_____
_____
_____

Chapter 2

The Young, Unguarded Heart

I cannot think of any need in childhood as strong as the need for the father's protection. —Sigmund Freud

One night, approximately one month before I turned fifteen, my older sister took me to a disco, and there I met the man who was to become my first husband. I was shy and nervous and didn't really want to be there. I stood around awkwardly trying to look cool, but feeling totally *uncool*. Suddenly, a guy came up and asked me if I wanted to dance. He was very tall and nice looking, but I said, "No, thank you." Five minutes later, another guy approached me and also asked me if I wanted to dance. As tall as the other guy was, this one was as short with shocking red hair, and I said, "Yes." We spent the next few hours dancing and getting to know one another. I found out later that the two of them were best friends and had made a bet to see who I'd say yes to!

At the end of the evening the redheaded guy offered to take me home, and I said yes. Actually, he just wanted to show off his car to me. It was a big deal for a guy to have a car in those days. It was an even bigger deal for the girlfriend of the guy who owned the car. We stopped at a garage for fuel, and while he was standing outside watching the gauge, I realized what I'd done by accepting a lift with a stranger, and men at that. I started to panic.

Oh, and did I mention that in the back seat of this tiny little Mini Cooper was his best friend? Yes, the same six-foot, six-inch guy who first asked me to dance? It turns out he was really shy and it had apparently taken him every ounce of courage to ask me to dance. I felt badly when I learned that, but only for ten seconds. (Sadly, Rob passed away many years ago, and I remember him now with fond memories).

Back to my panic. Looking back on that night, it was a dumb thing to do—getting into a car with two strange men I'd never laid eyes on before that night. And then I panicked even more when he dropped Rob off first and I realized we would be driving to my house on our own. I was a naïve, insecure teenager with rejection issues (although I didn't know that at the time). Nevertheless, somewhere in my crazy mixed up head I was enjoying the evening and was thinking of my fairy-tale dream. I'm going to fast forward my story for the moment.

THE FAIRY TALE

A few years ago I read a devotional written by Lynn Cowell from Proverbs 31 Ministries[1] and two of the questions she raised in her devotional were: "What do you wish for young people today?" "What is the one thing you wish you could tell them?"

Those are loaded questions and they played around in my head like a stuck record for weeks after I read them. Back then I didn't know anything about guarding my heart (Proverbs 4:23) or anything even remotely like that. To me it was a simple equation of: "Boy meets girl." "Boy likes girl." "Girl likes boy." "Boy wants girl." "Girl wants to be wanted." And in my young mind that all added up to love. How wrong I was.

That was back in 1972. The redheaded guy took me home and the inevitable happened. It's a time that I don't think about anymore, as it was a painful issue for me. Suffice to say, it was a traumatic ending to an evening that promised to be the start of something exciting. It was a painful experience; and unfortunately, also the night my dream was shattered and my heart broken. The night that my life with the fairy-tale ending ended. No more beautiful, innocent bride and cherished wife. And for some strange reason, I felt that I'd let my dad down. That our relationship would never be the same again. I'm not sure why that thought came to mind. It just did. But I've since dealt with the issues of that night and any regrets I had have now all been left in the past where they belong.

According to biblical thinking, two human beings who have shared the sexual act are never the same afterward. They can

no longer act toward each other as if they had not had this experience. It makes out of those involved in it a couple bound to each other. It creates a one-flesh bond with all its implications.
—Walter Trobisch[2]

The guy I met asked me to be his girlfriend, and I said yes. We started dating, but what should have been an exciting time became a battle between the sexes and a relationship challenge. I believe the reason is because on that fateful night that my dream died, something in my heart died too. I wasn't the same innocent young girl anymore. I was an angry, hurting person. This caused our relationship to be extraordinarily stormy. He was a jealous guy, and he wanted me to be his sole property. I, on the other hand, had decided that no one was ever going to tell me what to do again, and I fought that possessiveness with every ounce of strength I had. But here's the twist, I realized much later that I'm not the fighting type. In fact, my natural personality is happy, soft-hearted, caring. However, I'd changed and there was no going back.

Let's return to the question I read in Lynn Cowell's devotional: "What do you wish for young people today?" "What is the one thing you wish you could tell them?" In the Bible, in the Song of Solomon 2:7 (GW) it says, "Young women of Jerusalem, swear to me by the gazelles or by the does in the field that you will not awaken love or arouse love before its proper time."

And that verse sums up what my wish for young people is. The one thing I wish I could tell young people today. Awakening love before its proper time is like opening a fruit before it's ripe. The fruit is green, raw, immature, and not tasty if opened before its ripened state. On the other hand, experiments have revealed that "wounding" can stimulate ripening. Ancient Egyptians would gash figs. They noticed this would stimulate ripening. So even picking an unripe fruit can induce ripening.[3] I relate this analogy to my experience of wounding, which unfortunately stimulated ripening (premature maturing) in me.

But let's understand why a young girl wants to awaken love before its proper time in the first place. The answer to that question I learned many years after the event, but I believe the short and simple answer is that most young girls want the fairy tale. At least, that's what they think they want.

When the movie *Pretty Woman*, starring Richard Gere and Julia Roberts, first hit the screens (in March 1990), I'm sure I was one of the first at the theater to watch it. I was a romantic movie junkie, and I'm embarrassed to say that I watched it way too many times than I should have. The story line is the legendary rags to riches with Roberts playing the part of a prostitute and Gere rescuing her from a life on the streets. However, he didn't want marriage and commitment. What he did want to do was help her stay off the streets; and to that end, he arranged for her to have her own apartment, servants, credit cards, and anything else her heart desired. But, of course, her heart didn't desire material possessions. So when she turned him down and left town, he was puzzled. He wanted to know why she would give up that kind of dream life.

He went after her and asked her this question: "If you don't want the apartment, the servants, the money, and everything else I'm offering, then what exactly do you want?" To which she replied: "The fairy tale."

To Be Accepted, Loved, Cherished

So, what is the fairy tale? I believe it's what most young girls want— to be accepted, loved, and cherished. God has wired women that way. But the reality is that our teenagers want to know how to deal realistically and practically with confusing and insecurity issues that are so prevalent in today's society.

Some years ago, I was asked to look after two tweens when their parents went away for a week. I was quite intimidated by the task, and I asked a seasoned tween teacher what I could do with these two young girls for a week. She said I should do a role-playing interview with them. Find out what makes a tween girl tick. I drew up a list of questions and began to interview them in a fun way. They were fairly close in age, so I interviewed them together. Here's a sample of some questions I asked and their answers:

Me: "What do girls your age think about?"

Girls (in unison): "Boys."

Me: "Ok, anything else?"

Girls: "Yes" (giggling). "Boys."

All righty then, I was getting the message, loud and clear. Girls think about boys—A LOT! Thankfully I learned there are other things they think about apart from boys, like clothes, shopping, image and appearance, what's happening on social media, and peer perception.

The following are some other general statistics from teenage girls that I have read in various publications over the years:

> ➤ 62 percent of girls have noticed a guy they like and want to be his girlfriend in the fullest sense of the word.

> ➤ 74 percent of girls want to feel wanted and loved by a guy.

> ➤ 46 percent of girls think it's cute when they see young couples adoring one another.

These are not huge stats, but I have been around long enough to know (and I've raised two daughters myself), that girls are wired in a way that too easily draws them to boys like a magnet. They therefore need protection from themselves and they need to be educated as to why they need that protection. This is where the role of fathers is so important. I cannot do justice to this subject in a short chapter, nor am I qualified to do so, but I do want to emphasize to fathers that it is definitely not only in an ideal world that children, especially daughters, find safety under the love and protection of their father.

There really is no excuse today for parents to fob this duty off onto school teachers, parents of their children's friends, Sunday school teachers, other family members, and the like. There are innumerable resources available today for any parent wanting to raise their children in the way of the Lord.

And I encourage fathers in particular, to take their role of protector, provider, and head of the home as seriously as God intends them to. Your daughters need you to be their loving protectors, more than any other role. Will you rise to the occasion and take up the challenge?[4]

"BUT GOD" CHAPTER 2

The verses I've chosen for this chapter are Song of Solomon 2:7 and Proverbs 4:23.

If I allowed myself to have regrets, which I don't anymore, the biggest regret was believing the lie that love equals sex. I won't go so far as to say, I wish I'd never married my first husband because I did love him. Also, if I hadn't married him, I wouldn't have my daughters, sons-in-law, and grandchildren. And that's unthinkable. Not even negotiable. If I had my life again I wouldn't do that part differently. What I would do differently, however, is that first, I would never start dating or marry at such a young age. I would make a career for myself. Perhaps in law, journalism, or even a news anchor, a far cry from a secretary, but there you have it. These would be the different choices I would make.

If I had my way, I would definitely save myself (my virginity) until my wedding night, no matter what. And I would choose my friends more carefully. I would definitely have had more fun and done some adventurous stuff instead of being so stiff and serious.

I would have appreciated my parents and siblings more and done whatever it took to build better relationships with them.

These are a lot of "If onlys," but I share them with you for two reasons: (1) With the hope that they will help whoever reads this book to avoid similar regrets; but more importantly, (2) That every reader will know that even in the midst of shattered dreams, there is still a "But God." But God's grace was, still is, and always will be sufficient for all our needs. For His power is made perfect in weakness (see 2 Corinthians 12:9).

Nothing is ever wasted with God. He has used my life experiences, as difficult as they were, to minister over the years to many women and young girls. To let them know that He loves them with an unconditional love and that nothing will ever be able to separate them from His love (Romans 8:39). Recommended reading: Lynn Cowell's book, *His Redeeming Love*.

Let me repeat those two questions again and add a third one:

1. What do you wish for young people today?
2. What is the one thing you wish you could tell them?
3. What would you tell your young self if you had the chance?

Verses to Meditate on and Memorize from Chapter 2

> Song of Solomon 2:7 (GW): *Young women of Jerusalem, swear to me by the gazelles or by the does in the field that you will not awaken love or arouse love before its proper time.*

> Proverbs 4:23: *Guard your heart above all else; for it determines the course of your life.*

Journal your thoughts:

_____
_____
_____
_____
_____
_____
_____
_____

Journal your prayer:

_____
_____
_____
_____
_____
_____
_____
_____

ENDNOTES

1. www.proverbs31.org; www.lynncowell.com; accessed October 23, 2017.

2. Walter Trobisch, *I Married You* (Bolivar, MO: Quiet Waters Publications, 1971).

3. http://www.academia.edu/6927695/Fruit_Ripening_ How_Does_It_Work; accessed November 23, 2017.

4. I recommend any parenting (or marriage) resource by Dennis and Barbara Rainey or Focus on the Family: http://www.familylife.com or www.focusonthefamily. org; accessed October 23, 2017.

Chapter 3

Those Early Years

I think men who have pierced ears are better prepared for marriage. They've experienced pain and bought jewelry. –Rita Rudner

I remember reading one day in Bishop T.D. Jakes' book, *Woman Thou Art Loosed*[1], this statement: "If you are not complete as a person, marriage will not help you." But I wanted marriage, and I thought at the time that marriage would help me and more importantly, complete me. So, after a few years of unsuccessful dating (hello, if that wasn't a red flag then I don't know what was), a month after my 18th birthday my boyfriend and I got married. When I think about that today, it doesn't seem possible that I was married at the age of eighteen. Out of all my friends and my daughter's friends, not many married at that early age.

Even though getting married was all I'd ever wanted to do since the age of five, I had a sense on my wedding day that things might not turn out the way I hoped and expected. It didn't stop me though from pushing that thought out of my head, choosing rather to believe that our marriage would be exactly what I wanted. And anyway, the deed was done and I was raised in a church that did not believe in divorce. The marriage service was conducted, hymns sung, vows exchanged and register signed—there was no going back.

We were married in 1975 in the Catholic Church, a beautiful, white wedding. My aunt was a dressmaker and she made my stunning wedding gown, together with veil and six-foot (nearly two metre) train. She also made my bridesmaids' dresses and my mother's dress. My color scheme was pink and blue. We had three bridesmaids, a best man, and two groomsmen. Between my parents and in-laws, all the practical arrangements were made. We had the reception in the hall attached to the church. We hired the most popular and expensive five-piece band in Bulawayo and the catering was handled by the ladies from our church. All our family and friends were there to help celebrate this happy occasion; and for all intents and purposes, it was a picture-perfect wedding day.

But much to my regret, I don't remember much of the service or the day itself; it went by in a whirl of activity. I do remember, however, looking and feeling like a princess for that short time. Unfortunately, I also recall being a tad irritated that my husband kept accidentally standing on my train and each time he put his arm around me, my veil would slide down my back!

So much has happened since that day, and when I look back now, it seems like a million years ago. I'm very glad I have the memories to look back on. I've moved past the pain, but it was hard.

WRONG REASONS

I don't know when or how it came about when I realized shortly after we got married that I got married for all the wrong reasons. Love and marriage aren't always what they seem. Even in those days, particularly in those days, the media painted a romantic and idealistic picture of love and marriage, and that was so me—idealistic and a hopeless romantic. I really did believe in Prince Charming and happily-ever-after endings. But that unrealistic fairy-tale thinking soon came to a grinding halt as I began to live out real, practical, day-to-day married life, as it was.

At the time we got married I was working at a well-known engineering company. I was a junior shorthand secretary and I was good at my job. I was learning a lot in this first job of mine and I also had an excellent mentor. She was the private secretary who turned out to be one of my closest friends. She is still alive today (at the time of writing this book), although she now lives in Australia. She taught me so much about office and secretarial etiquette. In fact, because I felt so confident in my job, years later I wrote my own course manual on secretarial etiquette, which I've used over the years to train junior secretaries.

In my mind, however (and I'm being brave by making this statement), I always felt that married women and moms should be at home looking after their husbands and children—not working and making a career for themselves. I'll probably have women throw the book down in disgust after reading that comment, but I'm being honest; that is what I believed. And now I'm really being bold in saying that to some degree I still believe that; well at least until the children are school-going age.

THE HOUSEWIFE

At the time I left school, the most common careers for women were either a secretary, teacher, or nurse. Obviously, I chose the secretarial route. I was happy in my job, but a year after we were married, and even though I didn't have any reason to leave the workplace, and because of my convictions, I resigned from my job and became a housewife. I cannot even remember what I did to fill my days, because I wasn't a homemaker by any stretch of the imagination. I didn't have a clue about gardening. I couldn't sew or knit or do any other craft, and I couldn't cook to save my life. In fact, one day I decided I would try and impress my in-laws, particularly my mother-in-law (as she was a good old-fashioned, home-cooking woman) by inviting them over for Sunday lunch (which was usually held at my mother-in-law's house every week). As Rhodesia was under colonial rule, most people adopted typical British traditions, like roasts on Sundays with all the trimmings.

I bought the chicken, put it in the oven to roast, and made all the other dishes—veggies, rice, potatoes etc. The family arrived on time, suitably impressed with the way I'd taken on this challenge to host the family for a meal. The first thing I did was make a pot of tea. I put the tea-cozy on the teapot, set up the tea-tray, and carried it into the lounge. I'm not sure what happened, but the next thing I knew I stumbled and the tray, together with all its contents—teapot, milk jug, sugar bowl, cups and saucers—went flying. I was mortified.

That was embarrassment number one. After I had cleaned up the mess and made another tray of tea, we then sat down to lunch. It sure smelled good and it looked good too. I was really proud of myself.

The first real meal I'd ever made. I was sure my in-laws would be impressed too. We passed the plates around and my husband began carving the chicken. As he did so, the knife seemed to get stuck on something in the middle. He continued carving until the cavity was exposed and there sticking out of the cavity was a plastic bag with four chicken feet protruding through the bag, plus the raw giblets and livers!

I was crushed. But it was funny and everyone laughed, which broke the tension. Nevertheless, I never forgot that first attempt at entertaining. Unfortunately, what should have been an innocent mistake excused and forgotten, became a defining moment for everything I did thereafter in the kitchen. Sadly, that's how I saw it.

So, there I was a full-time housewife with nothing to do. At that time the country was at war and many homes were robbed of fathers, sons, and brothers. My husband, however, did not have to serve in the military, as three years before we were married he was involved in an accident at work, causing the loss of an eye; therefore, he was exempt from army call-ups. My father never served in the military either, due to his age. My father and my husband were, however, volunteers for police reservist duties and the neighborhood watch movement, which was a community initiative.

On the other hand, both my brothers and one of my brothers-in-law were called up for initial nine-month military training, which increased to twelve months and eventually eighteen months' service, and subsequent call-ups at six to eight weekly intervals, serving at the frontline borders.

It was a trying and challenging time for families in Rhodesia, and the constant army call-up system caused irreparable damage to many marriages and families. Sadly, it was common knowledge that the continual army call-up system would either "make or break" a marriage and family. I didn't have that excuse.

In 1977 we decided to start trying for a baby. I became pregnant almost straight away. Unfortunately, I lost the baby at about eight weeks. I became pregnant again shortly after that, but once again I miscarried, also at about eight weeks. When I became pregnant for a third time, our first daughter was born six months before my 21st birthday.

What a joy it was to be a mother; and because I wanted a daughter, it was a double joy.

Although I was an inexperienced mom, I still loved the role of motherhood. There was great excitement in the family when our first daughter was born, as she was the first granddaughter on my side of the family and the first on my husband's side of the family after many years. It was a wonderful celebration for both families.

Now I had this five-pound, three-ounce bundle of joy to pour my life into, which is what I did. I was so captivated by this baby. I thought I was doing quite well for a first-time mother, but when I look back now, I realize that I was clueless, neurotic, and obsessive, all wrapped up in one. I loved all the beautiful baby girl clothes that were available in the shops, and I would change her at least four times a day—just because I could.

The other obsessive thing I did was not allow anyone to hold her or even pick her up, except her father of course. By not allowing anyone to be involved in her life, she became so attached to me that she would scream if anyone got too close to her or even if anyone got in the car with us. However, I am relieved to tell you that we both eventually grew out of that and she grew up to be a beautiful normal woman who is now a wonderful mother herself.

Two and a half years after our daughter was born, I gave birth to a second daughter. She was also a beautiful little baby and so good. At that time, I unfortunately went into postnatal depression[2] that lasted about three months. It was a horrible time. I'm thankful that eventually I began to feel normal again.

Postnatal depression is very debilitating. It wasn't something I knew a lot about either, and I was therefore thankful that with the love and help of family and friends I got over it without any lasting consequences to either mom or daughter.

I am so grateful to the Lord that both my daughters have grown up to be exceptional women, wives, and mothers. It certainly was nothing that I did, because I was such a dysfunctional woman. God's grace covered us all long before we ever knew or acknowledged Him—what a wonderful and gracious God we serve!

"But God" Chapter 3

When I reread this chapter, I feel embarrassed and emotional, because of my obsessiveness and immaturity. But then, I tell myself that I'm not the first clueless mom, and I know I won't be the last! I've also gained knowledge along the way, which I can pass on to other young women who can gain perspective and hope as they struggle with similar issues.

Because of what happened to me at that tender age of fourteen, I never had the teenager experiences that normal teenagers enjoy. I was an adult in a child's body and was always serious and disapproving of teenagers clowning around. I realized, though, that deep down inside, I wanted to do the same. I also had such unrealistic expectations of marriage and home life. I imagined making my home a place that was warm, welcoming, and aesthetically beautiful.

I was devastated to find that I had no creativity in that department and quite frankly I didn't have a clue what I was good at. I found marriage and homemaking to be unstimulating and mundane. Quite the opposite of what I thought it would be.

I loved being a mom, but I didn't have anyone to share that with until my daughters started nursery school and I met other mothers. I was also awkward around other mothers, not knowing what to do and what to teach my children. If only I'd known then what I know now. But there's no room for regrets, so let's move on to the "But God."

As I prayed about what God wanted me to put into this chapter, He brought to mind Mary, Jesus' mother. Apparently Mary was only about fourteen years of age when the angel Gabriel appeared to her with the message that she was favored among all women, to be the mother of Jesus. We know from the Scriptures that she was confused, disturbed, and afraid (Luke 1). What did she know about being a mom and the mother of the Messiah? Not much I'm sure, and at that age, didn't she also have teenage dreams? She was, after all, betrothed to Joseph.

Solomon tells us in Ecclesiastes 1:9-10 (Contemporary English Version) that there's nothing new under the sun. Everything that's being done now has been done before, "Everything that happens has happened before; nothing is new, nothing under the sun. Someone might say, 'Here is something new!' But it happened before, long before we were born."

I was an insecure mom and I've always had a hang-up about that. "But God" showed me that Mary, the woman chosen to birth the Messiah, was probably no different from other insecure moms. Do I feel better now? You bet I do! And if you have also felt inadequate and insecure as a young mom, you can take comfort too.

What stands out for you in those early years of motherhood? What did you excitedly expect that turned out to be disappointingly opposite? And on the other end of the spectrum, what did you expect would be hard that surprised you and turned out to be something you were good at?

Verses to Meditate on and Memorize from Chapter 3

➤ Proverbs 2 The Benefits of Wisdom: *My child, listen to what I say, and treasure my commands. Tune your ears to wisdom, and concentrate on understanding. Cry out for insight, and ask for understanding. Search for them as you would for silver; seek them like hidden treasures. Then you will understand what it means to fear the Lord, and you will gain knowledge of God. For the Lord grants wisdom! From his mouth come knowledge and understanding. He grants a treasure of common sense to the honest. He is a shield to those who walk with integrity. He guards the paths of the just and protects those who are faithful to him.*

Then you will understand what is right, just, and fair, and you will find the right way to go. For wisdom will enter your heart, and knowledge will fill you with joy. Wise choices will watch over you. Understanding will keep you safe.

Wisdom will save you from evil people, from those whose words are twisted. These men turn from the right way to walk down dark paths. They take pleasure in doing wrong, and they enjoy the twisted ways of evil. Their actions are crooked, and their ways are wrong. Wisdom will save you from the immoral woman, from the seductive words of the promiscuous woman. She has abandoned her husband and ignores the covenant she made before God. Entering her house leads to death; it is the road to the grave. The man who visits her is doomed. He will never reach the paths of life. So follow the steps of the good, and stay on the paths of the righteous. For only the godly will live in the land, and those with integrity will remain in it. But the wicked will be removed from the land, and the treacherous will be uprooted.

➤ Titus 2:3-5 (GNT): *In the same way instruct the older women to behave as women should who live a holy life. They must not be slanderers or slaves to wine. They must teach what is good, in order to train the younger women to love their husbands and children, to be self-controlled and pure, and to be good housewives who submit themselves to their husbands, so that no one will speak evil of the message that comes from God.*

Journal your thoughts:

_____

_____

_____

_____

_____

_____

_____

Journal your prayer:

_____

_____

_____

_____

_____

_____

_____

ENDNOTE

1. T. D. Jakes, *Woman, Thou Art Loosed* (Shippensberg, PA: Treasure House, 1994).

2. "The arrival of a new baby is usually a happy event, but it can also be a stressful time during which many adjustments must be made. Many women are not aware that mood changes are common after childbirth and vary from mild to severe. In fact, in the year after childbirth a woman is more likely to need psychiatric help than at any time in her life. There are three recognised mood disorders in the postpartum period. At one end of the spectrum is 'baby blues', affecting about 80 per cent of new mothers, almost expected by all mothers. It usually occurs between the third and tenth day after birth. Symptoms include tearfulness, anxiety, mood fluctuations and irritability. The 'blues' are transient and will pass with understanding and support."

Excerpt from MyDr, *Postnatal depression: what is it?* http://www.mydr.com.au/babies-pregnancy/postnatal-depression-what-is-it; accessed October 24, 2017.

Chapter 4

The Foolish Woman
Tore Down Her House

If you don't receive love from the ones who are meant to love you, you will never stop looking for it. –Robert Goolrick

So, I'm in the church at the altar repeating these words: "I, Leonie, take you Trevor, to be my lawfully wedded husband, to have and to hold from this day forward, for better, for worse, for richer, for poorer, in sickness and in health, to love and to cherish; until death do us part." The thought never crossed my mind that one day I would repeat these very same words—two more times in my life!

To my mind, love meant getting married. In fact, our wedding invitation had these words on the front: "Love is...getting married." But I just wanted the "for better" and "love and cherish" parts. All my longings, dreams, and desires were based on marriage and what marriage could and would do for me, or so I naively thought. I was obsessed with the idea of love and marriage. In this chapter, I talk about the expectations I had regarding the role of a husband.

When I look back now and knowing what I know today, the expectations I had of the role of a husband were just plain unrealistic. In retrospect, I also think those expectations came from my perspective of my parents' marriage. My parents celebrated 62 years of marriage on February 14, 2015, and up until the age of forty-two, I thought my parents had the perfect marriage. I thought my dad was about as perfect a husband and father that any wife could find.

When my parents celebrated their 50th wedding anniversary, their story was featured in the local paper. When the interviewer asked my mother why she loved my father and had stayed married to him for so long, without hesitation she replied, "Because he has always been a gentleman and a kind, loving, gentle man. He has also worked hard and provided for his family all his life."

And therein was the reason why I wanted to get married. However, having said that, I failed to take into account the "everydayness" of love and marriage. In other words, I wanted the "for better" and not the "for worse" part, which is obviously not possible. Unfortunately, I know that today. I didn't know that back then. My shattered expectations left me hopelessly discouraged and disappointed, so much so that I went into a deep depression that totally overwhelmed me.

I was always an avid reader growing up. It was about the only subject I really liked at school, apart from history and domestic science (known as home economics today), and I excelled at it. I never read educational or informative books in those days, as I do today. Instead, I immersed myself in stupid, soppy, romance novels with fairy-tale endings. I became addicted to books of this genre. As I filled my mind with rubbish, my expectations of love and marriage became more and more warped as time went on. Eventually the inevitable happened. I could not continue reading that type of junk without it playing out in real life. I became dissatisfied with my marriage and thoughts of divorce began to fill my mind.

I justified to myself that if I got divorced there was still a chance that I could have the dream marriage and live the dream life. I was still young. There was still time. The fact that my conscience convicted me that divorce was wrong on every level, did not change the way I thought. Even the fact that my husband and children would be devastated didn't stop me from thinking about it anyway. I now understand, which I didn't then, how our thoughts control our actions, and at some stage, if we continue to entertain such thoughts, they will become a reality. I continued to fantasize about how my life could be. In reality, however, the only thing that happened was that my life was on a self-destruct mission destined for disaster.

SELF-DESTRUCTION MISSION

After some months passed, I approached my husband one night and told him that I wanted a divorce. He was obviously taken aback, as he had not seen anything like that coming. We got into a heated argument, as he tried to convince me that this course of action was the worst possible thing I could do. He asked me to reconsider the repercussions of what my decision would do to us, and especially our daughters. He said this was just a whim on my part and a selfish one at that.

I did consider it for days, weeks, even months, but the thought of a new life became like an addiction, and I couldn't let it go. I knew there would be devastating consequences, but I didn't know how to stop it. And so, after a period of time, the subject came up again, and this time I told him that I meant to go through with my decision, no matter what. He didn't argue with me this time. He did ask me if I would at least consider a trial separation and marriage counseling before I sought an outright divorce, which I agreed to.

We found a marriage counselor and began counseling. In my mind I felt we were just going around in circles and not really getting to the root of the problem. I used to think and believe that marriage was a 50-50 thing, but I learned much later that it's actually a 100-100 thing. While I wrote this chapter, it gave me the opportunity to reflect once again on the hurt and anger my husband must have felt. Even now, it feels intense. It feels raw. It feels hard. We did separate eventually. He moved out of the house but let me continue living there with the children.

Leaving the home did not stop my husband from leaving me alone. As a result, we ended up seeing each other almost every day. I knew this would happen. The children were confused. He was upset. And I hid behind my decision. While we were separated, I went to see a lawyer about going through with the divorce, and he didn't discourage me in any way. What he did do was spell out the legal aspects of the divorce. I was satisfied and instructed him to go ahead and draw up the papers. My husband and I then had a meeting with the lawyer to go over the contents of the divorce order. My husband indicated the changes he wanted made. I agreed to all the changes. Anything for it all to be over, as quickly as possible.

The court date was set and the day dawned with a heavy cloud hanging over me. We sat in a dark, unfriendly courtroom waiting for our number to be called. Eventually it was our turn. The judge read the papers in front of him and then something quite unexpected happened. The judge said he was not prepared to grant the divorce, as there was not sufficient justification for it. He ordered a period of counseling for six months and would review the case thereafter. I couldn't believe what I heard. I had prepared myself mentally, physically, and emotionally. I would now have to do it all over again in six months' time.

The judge's decision had the opposite effect on my husband. He was elated and said that he knew I had made the wrong decision in the first place. He said maybe this time-out was what I needed to rethink my rash decision. I agreed to do what I was ordered to do, but inside I was as determined as ever to go through with the divorce.

We went back to the marriage counselor and told him what the judge had said. He tried his very best to help us get our marriage back on track. It just wasn't working, and I knew I was the stumbling block. I was not prepared to compromise and do the work that needed to be done.

TORN DOWN

Obviously, I'm writing this book in retrospect realizing that the problems in our marriage were not caused by my husband or anything he did or did not do, although I agree it takes two to make a marriage work. I do believe, however, that our problems were predominantly due to my dysfunction, fairy-tale thoughts, and unrealistic expectations. My decision to divorce my husband was unfortunately not based on rational thinking; nor did I have eternity in mind, which is of paramount importance.

I titled this chapter "The Foolish Woman Tore Down Her House," which comes from Proverbs 14:1 that says, "A wise woman builds her home, but a foolish woman tears it down with her own hands." And I am sad to say, that is what I did. Exactly six months after our first trip to the divorce courts, we found ourselves back again before the magistrate. This time he did grant the divorce. That was twenty-nine years ago. A long time, and yet I remember that day as if it were yesterday. Thirteen years of marriage and it took less than thirteen minutes to end it all. With heavy hearts we went our separate ways that fateful day agreeing to stay friends for the sake of the children.

It's been my observation that divorced women unfortunately carry a stigma. The *US English Thesaurus* says that stigma means shame, disgrace, dishonor, and humiliation. I thought divorce would make me feel free and alive. What I actually felt was shameful, disgraceful, dishonored, and humiliated. The days, weeks, months, and years that followed my divorce were difficult, painful, and full of regret.

My ex-husband and I placed huge demands on one another. He insisted on seeing the children every second weekend. He wanted to see them every weekend, but practically that was not possible, as he lived away from Johannesburg, where the girls and I lived. We agreed that he would see the children two weekends a month and alternate holidays. On the weekends when it was his turn to see the children, I would take them to his house, which was about 280 kilometers (174 miles) away, which I resented having to do. Most of the time I was not up for the argument, so I gave in to his demands.

ONE BIG MESS

Sometimes when I dropped off the children and saw him, I hated him and was glad we weren't together anymore. At other times I still loved him and wished we were still married. My emotions were all over the place. In fact, we did get back together at one time, but it only lasted a few months, and eventually it got to the stage where there were too many bad memories and we really had to walk away and close the door completely in order to move on with our respective lives.

Throughout this process the children were understandably angry and extremely hurt. When I left their father, I promised them that their standard of living wouldn't change and that we would have some really fun times together in our new life. However, it is foolish to make promises I couldn't fulfill, because it wasn't fun or wonderful, and our standard of living went down, drastically.

It's been my experience that, generally, divorced women tend to struggle financially. They also become tired and burdened by all the extra responsibilities they have to shoulder alone. In addition, they sometimes take on the role of mother and father, which is not conducive to a wonderful, fun-filled life, nor is it good for the children not to have their father around.

What I want to highlight is that my children were desperately unhappy and their unhappiness eventually became the glasses they would use to view life and relationships, as they grew into adult women themselves. Both of them had been hurt deeply and acted out that hurt in the course of life. I was also ill-equipped to deal with two teenage girls while my life was so out of control. It was just one big mess!

In order to do justice to the subject of the pain and hurt children experience through a divorce and to quote accurate statistics and facts, I would need to write another book; and to that end, I hope to do just that in the not too distant future. However, for the purpose of this chapter, I will just say that I cannot emphasize enough the damage that is done to children through the trauma of divorce.

I realize that people choose divorce for many reasons, and we will talk about this topic more as we go into the book. Suffice to say that my girls and I have cried many tears over my decision to divorce their father. It impacted their lives as they grew up and began their own independent lives, and we all bear the scars even to this day.

"But God" Chapter 4

As you will find out later in the book, I only started to know the Bible in my early 40s. I'm not making excuses for the divorce, but I must say that if I knew then what I know now, I believe my decision to divorce would have been different. The Scripture that comes to mind is in 1 Corinthians 10:23. Paul is writing to the church in Corinth warning them about idol worship, and he tells them that "'I am allowed to do anything'—but not everything is beneficial." In other words, you and I can get divorced if we want to, but is it beneficial?

"But God" says we cannot go back. We must forget the former things and look at the new things that He has begun in us. I want to reiterate, as I do quite extensively in the following pages, that divorce for me was devastating and destructive for everyone involved.

I was preparing for a talk once and I read somewhere in my research that apparently sixteen people are affected through one divorce, and that number multiplies if one of those sixteen people gets divorced and so on. That's a huge number and a lot of unhappy and broken people.

A dear friend of mine, Mrs. Bev van Rensburg, wrote a thesis for her Master's degree entitled "Children in Crisis in South Africa", with emphasis on the need for both the physical father and the heavenly Father to be present in the home. I realize that sometimes that is just not possible for a number of reasons. Bev said this after writing her thesis: "When I finished my thesis on Children in Crisis in South Africa, I was convinced that we have to teach at the grassroots level on the Father-heart of God in the home and on sexual purity, especially to teenagers and marginalized children and carers." Bev has also written two booklets on those topics entitled *Where Are You, Father?* and *Destined for Pure Love*. These invaluable resources are available from Bev. For more information, please email her at bev@sats.edu.za if you would like a copy of either.

Verses to Mediate on and Memorize from Chapter 4:

➤ Malachi 2:16: *"I hate divorce," says the Lord, the God of Israel....*

➤ Matthew 19:6 (GNT): *So they are no longer two, but one. No human being must separate, then, what God has joined together.*

Journal your thoughts:

_____

_____

_____

_____

_____

_____

_____

_____

_____

Journal your prayer:

_____

_____

_____

_____

_____

_____

_____

_____

_____

_____

Chapter 5

The Blind Date

I now realize that lives fall apart when they need to be rebuilt. Lives fall apart when the foundation upon which they were built needs to be re-laid. Lives fall apart, not because God is punishing us for what we have or have not done. Lives fall apart because they need to. They need to because they weren't built the right way in the first place. –Iyanla Vanzant

I was now a free woman, though still an unhappy one. In fact, if anything, I felt even worse than before. I was depressed and I spent most of my time sleeping, just so I could get enough energy to function from day to day. By this time, I had secured a good job and I was spending long hours at work. I think I was trying to make a success of something in my life, and my job seemed to be the one place I could do that.

At this stage in my life I was so grateful for the wonderful friends I had who helped me take the girls to and from school and extramural activities. I also had a wonderful caring helper, Sarah, who helped me with domestic chores and with the practicalities of raising two young girls as a single, working mom.

Shortly after the divorce, a friend decided it would be a great idea to set me up with a blind date. Married friends always want to do the match-making thing when they have single friends. I'm not sure why they do this. Maybe so there'll be a foursome again, or maybe it's just that they don't want their friend(s) to be on their own or lonely. Whatever the reason, I was certainly not enthralled with the idea; it was far too soon for my liking. Plus, I liked to be the one in control, not vice versa. I agreed, however, to go on this one date only. Well, one date turned into two and two turned into three and then three turned into a full-blown courtship. My blind date fell madly in love with me on sight and proposed on the second date!

He was quite a charmer and liked to wine and dine me. I must say I enjoyed the royal treatment; nevertheless I was wary. I was not over my ex-husband, and the pain of divorce was still raw. At the same time, I thoroughly enjoyed being spoiled, and once again I allowed the dream world to cloud my emotions.

He had two teenage children, and at first our children got on well. However, once my children realized things were getting serious between us, they started pulling back and didn't want me to continue the relationship. His children, on the other hand, wanted the opposite. They were ready to adopt me early in the relationship, and his daughter even started calling me mom shortly after our first meeting. It was flattering and scary at the same time. I didn't know how to deal with teenagers, and I was way out of my league when it came to dealing with boys. My boyfriend, on the other hand, was patient and accommodating. He tried everything to win the girls over to his side. It didn't work. They were wary and torn between accepting his friendship and the love and loyalty to their father.

MARRIAGE NUMBER TWO

Eventually, however, I agreed to marry him, and a year and a half after the divorce, I got married for the second time. We bought a house together and in the beginning had all four children living with us full time. What a nightmare! My husband had his own business, and I was still working as a personal assistant. Our lives were full, busy, and tiring. With the freedom of his own business, my husband took on the role of "housekeeper and mom's taxi." He did the school runs, the extramural activities, and even visits to the ex-spouses. He also cooked, cleaned, shopped, and spent most nights doing the ironing, as I was exhausted from putting in long hours at work.

In order to maintain our sanity, we arranged for the children to visit their respective parents on the same weekends, which gave us some space and time for ourselves. However, as much as my husband was a kind, loving, and caring husband, I was so full of guilt and unhappiness that I would spend most of the time sleeping or crying—sometimes both. At the same time, I was constantly aware that my children were unhappy, and it weighed heavily on my heart. At times, I would feel so sad that I thought of taking my life. However, I also knew I could not do that to my children and loved ones.

Obviously, there are marriages the second time around that manage to achieve some measure of success. This wasn't the case for me. Blending or merging families was one of the hardest things I have ever had to do, and I never felt as though I had achieved even a small amount of success in that area. I admire people who get it right, but I struggled every day of my second marriage. Looking back, I believe the biblical view of marriage was so ingrained in me that I just could not accept step-families as being natural and normal. In addition, the fact that my children were also battling with this step-family they found themselves in, did not help matters.

Many years after I got divorced, I was at a conference where step-families were being discussed. I sensed God say to me that "step" and "half" were unnatural terms to refer to people. A step-mom, step-dad, step-brother or sister, for example, was really saying, "You're a step-away" from being a mom, dad, brother or sister; that you don't quite make the grade; and a half-brother or half-sister was actually saying, "You're only half a brother (man/boy) or half a sister (woman/girl)." Since that day, I never could refer to step-families and half-brothers and half-sisters without thinking of what God showed me.

CONSTANT CONFLICT

At this stage, my girls were moving into adolescence and everything that goes with that change and the older teens were pushing for more freedom. I found myself torn between my girls and my husband more often than I wanted to be. I chose to put my girls first, which caused tension between my husband and me.

With four emerging teenagers in the house, there was constant tension and conflict, which was tiring. The children also wanted to see their friends rather than go to their respective parents for the weekend, which meant my husband and I had to chaperone, chauffeur, and supervise children all weekend, leaving no time for the two of us. It wasn't long before the pressure and stress of trying to blend two families and remain sane began to take its toll on everyone. My husband and I began arguing and dividing more and more as each day passed.

Eventually, after three years of marriage, a lot of talking and debate, much to our disappointment, we both agreed that we couldn't continue in the marriage and opted for an amicable D-I-Y divorce. There were no disruptions and it was over in a flash. I was done! No, I was undone!

DONE AND UNDONE

Three years of hard work. Three years of plowing through endless baggage, and it ended quicker than it began. Now I was left with even more baggage and a very heavy heart. I didn't need an expert to tell me that I needed to do some serious soul-searching. I was close to a breakdown and full of self-condemnation. I had no idea what to do with my life and the question "where to from here" played over and over in my mind with no answer.

I lived from day to day and threw myself into work, which kept me busy and stopped me from thinking of what a mess I'd made of my life and the lives of the two most precious people in my life—my daughters. Unfortunately, I also fell into some pretty destructive relationships, thinking they would help me get over my second failed marriage. But all that did was make me feel even worse about myself than I did before (if that was possible). I was back on that vicious cycle.

God really does hate divorce as it says in Malachi 2:16, because it is devastating to everyone involved. I don't believe anything good comes from divorce, especially when children are involved, as they suffer the most. I don't have accurate statistics, nonetheless it is a known fact that

South Africa has one of the highest divorce rates in the world and that means a lot of unhappy, emotionally scarred people.

There is, however, a wonderful course that has been helping people for many years called DivorceCare (incorporating DivorceCare for Kids). You can find more information about this amazing course on their Website.[1] I was introduced to DivorceCare many years ago (after my second divorce), but for some reason I never took the course. Recently I realized why—I believed the lie that I did not *deserve* divorce care, as I was the one who had caused the divorces.

Quite sad really. God did not condemn me. That was a lie straight from the pit of hell! But the really sad part is that if I had known that was a lie, I would have disregarded it, joined the course class, which would have made a huge difference in my life, and would have given me the tools I needed to help my daughters too. If you are reading this book and feel you don't deserve God's grace and love, please do not believe that lie. Join a course right now! Do it for yourself. Do it for your children. Do it for your future.

DIFFICULTIES AND DEMANDS

Back to my life after divorce number two. It was a difficult time for all of us. Financially, I was struggling to make ends meet. The demands from school (apart from school fees), were never-ending. The girls were growing and they were becoming conscious of wearing brand-name clothing like their friends did, whose parents could afford to buy them the latest fashions. I began to give in to their demands, as I didn't want them to feel left out—and before long I found myself deep in debt. The thought of going to the divorce maintenance courts to receive an increase in my monthly stipend was too difficult, as it meant taking time off work, which wasn't easy. There was no guarantee that my case would be heard the same day anyway. I believe many women in this position think the same way. They tolerate their circumstances because they are too difficult to change. However, out of sheer desperation, I did go to the courts one day and managed to get a small increase, which helped ease the burden for a while.

All in all, my life as a divorcée was hard and a daily pretense, which took its toll on my health and emotional well-being. I would put on a happy and confident face in front of people, but deep down inside I was dying. I became a people-pleaser so I would be accepted and not shunned because I was divorced. If you're a people-pleaser, too, you know that the mask never comes off and living a lie is fraught with anxiety and fear, which is not at all conducive to healthy living.

"But God" Chapter 5

In the year 2000, I spoke at a marriage prep course on the difficulties of divorce, remarriage, and the merging of families. I had done some research and found the results of a survey that showed by the year 2010 there would be more step-families than natural families. That statistic shocked me, and I remember thinking, *God, if You will give me the opportunity, I'll be your mouthpiece to the world on the devastation and destruction of the family because of divorce.*

I'm not saying that it is impossible to merge families successfully. What I am saying is that for blended families to be successful, families, husbands, and wives need to invest time and effort God's way. Many couples honestly believe they will do just that, but it has been my experience that their initial conviction does not stand the test of time for many different reasons, mainly that it takes selfless dedication. By the time most families get to the crisis state, not many people in the family want to do the hard work.

The "But God" gem in this summary comes from Proverbs 15:22 (NKJV) "Without counsel, plans go awry, but in the multitude of counselors they are established." Use wisdom and get counsel from different sources. Enlist the help of family, friends, and your church, if you have one. Listen to your children's pain and do what needs to be done to ground and stabilize your new family.

Verses to Meditate on and Memorize from Chapter 5

> James 1:5 (GW): *If any of you needs wisdom to know what you should do, you should ask God, and he will give it to you. God is generous to everyone and doesn't find fault with them.*

> James 1:19 (GNT): *Remember this, my dear friends! Everyone must be quick to listen, but slow to speak and slow to become angry.*

Journal your thoughts:

_____
_____
_____
_____
_____
_____
_____
_____
_____

Journal your prayer:

_____
_____
_____
_____
_____
_____
_____
_____

ENDNOTE

1. If you want to enroll in DivorceCare, you will most probably find a course being offered at most local churches in your area. Find DivorceCare on the Internet: http://www. divorcecare.org/findagroup/countries/za and https://www. divorcecare.org/startagroup/dc4k; accessed October 24, 2017.

Chapter 6

The Beginning of the End

Sometimes it takes a painful experience to make us change our ways. —Proverbs 20:30 (GNT)

A week after I was divorced the second time, I went to visit family in Mauritius who were living there at the time. The day after I arrived, I was lying on the beach thinking to myself, *This time a week ago I was in the divorce courts in Johannesburg. Now a week later I'm on a beach in one of the most idyllic islands in the world.* What a contrast! I did a lot of thinking and soul searching those three weeks that I was away, yet nothing made sense to me. I couldn't understand how my life had sunk into such a mess. Why had it all gone so wrong?

I came from a good home. We weren't wealthy and we weren't particularly demonstrative in our affections toward one another. In fact, we hardly ever embraced or expressed our love and affection. We certainly didn't know anything about the five love languages, or counseling and therapy—not as we know it today—but it wasn't a bad home. Nevertheless, something had definitely happened to me leading up to the time when I became a young teenager; and whatever it was succeeded in convincing me that I wasn't loved or accepted, that I was an outcast, that I didn't fit in with the in-crowd. And that shift in my thinking caused my behavior to change, which contributed negatively to the way I viewed and lived my life from that time onward.

I thought that in order to be loved and accepted, I had to be a people-pleaser. That didn't work. The more I tried pleasing people, the more I had to please people. And the more I had to please people, the more pressure I felt; and that made me feel even worse about myself than I already did.

Unfortunately, because I was constantly trying to please people, I got entangled in a web of destructive relationships where I found it difficult to distinguish between love and infatuation. I didn't know how to get out or how to stop it. It was an unhealthy situation, and the only way to describe how I felt is to say that it was like living someone else's life. After three weeks' holiday in Mauritius, I returned home feeling rested and determined in my mind that I was going to turn my life around.

Four months after I returned from holiday, two men came into my life simultaneously. One of the two would become my third husband. This was not immediate, though; there was a long road ahead of us before that would happen. I met my husband-to-be quite by chance one day when he came into our offices while on a round of cold-calling to the companies in the building where I worked. Although I never spoke to him, I recognized him from my hometown, Bulawayo, and followed up with a phone call to him later that day. We had known each other in Rhodesia, and I had even attended school with his ex-wife. He was surprised but delighted to hear from me and after catching up on the years since we had last seen one another, he asked me out on a date. I accepted. We had an enjoyable night out with lots of reminiscing; and at the end of the evening, we made plans to see each other again.

The following week before I could go out with him again, a friend asked me if I would like to go with her to a hiking meeting, as she was thinking of signing up for a hike over a long weekend and wanted me to join her. I agreed and enjoyed what I heard that evening so much that I decided to join her the following weekend on the hike. I was introduced to the leader of the hike at that meeting and there was an instant attraction for both of us. Dave (not his real name) was the other man I mentioned earlier.

Dave and I got on really well, and by the end of the weekend we were keen to see each other again. He called me in the week and we went on a date. He asked me that night if I would be his girlfriend and I said yes. Needless to say my future husband was not happy. We did remain friends though.

Dave and I began dating. He was one of those guys most parents would want their daughters to marry. He was an easy-going and caring person.

A real gentleman. As we became better acquainted with each other, I observed that he was a great father too. We also had similar backgrounds in that he had been married twice before and had three sons from two marriages. He also came from Rhodesia—from my birthplace, Umtali.

His children took up a great deal of his spare time, and I tried to be understanding about that. However, it caused tension between us, as he wanted to spend time with his children alone so as not to confuse them. I needed to respect his decision, because he was doing the right thing. Nevertheless, it was hard not to see him most weekends.

The relationship was all that I had ever wanted. However, our individual issues were getting in the way. Attempts to juggle kids, ex-spouses, visits, holidays, lack of money, and little couple time, took a toll on us both. We agreed then, that as much as we loved each other and the last thing we wanted was to the end the relationship, the relationship was not sustainable. We were both devastated, but realized that if we continued dating, we would wind up hating each other, or our respective children, or both! We also decided not to even remain friends, as we might be tempted to get back together again and we knew that would be a big mistake.

An End and a Beginning

Toward the end of that year, my future husband and I got back together again, and that was the beginning of a very stormy eight-year courtship. From day one, Kevin and I had a love-hate relationship. We were both jealous and possessive of one another and as much as we didn't want to be apart, we also wanted our freedom and independence.

Kevin had married in his late twenties. The marriage was brief and ended in divorce. They never had children. At that time he had also been on the frontline border in the Rhodesian army; and over and above his initial military service of twelve months, he served in camps for six weeks in and ten days out, continuously for over a year. There was no time to build a marriage relationship, and it was no surprise to either of them, even though he was disappointed, when the eighteen-month marriage ended shortly after his thirtieth birthday. Kevin then proceeded to live the life of a carefree bachelor until we met many years later.

He obviously had other relationships in between his divorce and meeting me, but they were easy-going and fleeting. The company he kept were predominantly single males, and the pub was their frequent hangout. When we started dating, I was told quite emphatically that this was his routine and he wasn't about to change it for anyone, including me. I wasn't enthusiastic about that, as you can imagine. I did, however, accept his *fait accompli*; and to be honest, I thought he had the makings of a great husband, and I was going to be the one to make that happen! Little did I know that I was about to take on one of the most difficult challenges I'd ever faced. Not that I knew that back then—I'm speaking in retrospect twenty years down the line. I didn't know that he was as dysfunctional as I was and carried as much baggage, maybe even more, than I did.

DYSFUNCTIONAL CO-DEPENDENTS

We were also (unbeknown to either of us), co-dependent people. I had never heard of that term until many years later. To be co-dependent meant for us that subconsciously I was looking for someone to "fix and rescue," and he was looking to be "fixed and rescued"—hence the instant attraction.

When we met, I was single and my two daughters were living with me. He was also single and living in his own home not too far from where I lived. At some stage in our relationship, he sold his home and we moved in together. From the first day we began living together, I realized that I had a real challenge on my hands with Kevin. So, I did what any girl would do, I started trying to change him; and the more I tried to change him, the more he wouldn't be changed and the angrier I got. It was a vicious cycle.

Kevin was carrying a lot of anger, and we realized later that the root of his anger was due predominantly from years of peer rejection in junior school, and his subsequent lengthy time in the army.

The very last thing Kevin wanted to do was to get caught up in a war, and I'm sure there were many men who felt the same way. His reluctance to engage in active military service and the atrocities he had to see and endure for years while in combat caused deep-rooted anger, which he carried for many years.

There was continuous tension and conflict in our home, and neither of us was equipped to deal with conflict resolution. To me it was simple. I was right and he was wrong, and if he changed, everything would be fine. Kevin also thought it was simple—he didn't care whether he was right or wrong, take it or leave it. Still and all, four years after we started dating, on Valentine's Day 1998, he asked me to marry him. He took me away for the weekend, produced a stunning engagement ring, and proposed one night over dinner. I accepted. We set a date and I immediately began making plans.

Breakup and Breakdown

What should have been a happy time for me, wasn't. We argued about everything from the guest list to the cake and the dress to the venue. We couldn't agree on anything. I was suffering with depression and burnout, and six months later, I felt that I could not go through with the wedding. I gave back his ring. Told him I never wanted to see him again. Then I had a breakdown!

I literally went to pieces; and with the help of my sister and a friend, I went away for a week on my own. I had no way of communicating with anyone and I had no means of transportation either. Every day I would go for a walk, sit on top of a mountain, and just think. I thought about my life and all the bad decisions I'd made. I thought about all the many wrong relationships I was in over the years. I thought about the two divorces that shattered my life, shattered the lives of my children, and shattered the lives of my ex-husbands. I thought about my work situation. I thought about my horrendous financial situation and huge debt. More importantly, I thought about my relationship with Kevin and our future life together. Did we even have a future life together? Each night I would pray. But let me qualify "pray."

I didn't know anything about prayer in those days (except the Lord's Prayer). In 1988, my ex-husband and I went on holiday to the UK, Holland, and Belgium. It was the first time we'd been overseas, and it was an exciting time for us. One day while we were in Antwerp, we visited a cathedral. At the entrance were a pile of tracts with a prayer on them. The prayer said something to the effect that, if I prayed to (whoever the person was, I don't remember) every day for 100 days, I would get an answer to my prayers. For whatever reason, I kept that tract all those years, and I took it along with me to the place I went to think. I prayed that prayer many times every day during that week. You have to understand, though, that I had no idea what I was doing. I prayed that prayer out of total ignorance—to an "Unknown God," as Paul says in Acts 17:22-23 (NKJV):

> *Then Paul stood in the midst of the Areopagus and said, "Men of Athens, I perceive that in all things you are very religious; for as I was passing through and considering the objects of your worship, I even found an altar with this inscription: TO THE UNKNOWN GOD. Therefore, the One whom you worship without knowing, Him I proclaim to you.*

That week on my own soon came to an end. I sent a message to Kevin to fetch me, which he did. I was still in a bad place emotionally and I cannot tell you that anything miraculous or supernatural happened to me, or even that my situation changed in any way. It didn't. What I did experience, however, was a restlessness that I can't explain. All I knew was that somewhere deep inside me I knew I couldn't continue to live the way I had been living up to that time.

Something had to change. I began to experience a deep longing for something to happen to change my life for the better. That was in August 1998; and unbeknown to me, I was about to have my desire come true!

"But God" Chapter 6

"To everything there is a season; a time for every purpose under heaven," so says King Solomon in Ecclesiastes 3:1 (NKJV), where he also says, "There is a time to weep and a time to laugh; a time to mourn, and a time to dance" (Ecclesiastes 3:4 NKJV). Well, my time of weeping and mourning was over. It was nearing time to laugh and dance!

People do strange things, even wicked things, and we judge them, although we don't always verbalize the judgment. We decide in our minds who measures up and who doesn't. If I had known "Leonie" in those early days, I probably would have been one of the first to judge her harshly, because of the life she lived.

"But God" thankfully does not judge by outward appearance. He looks at the heart of a person and He knew that my heart was aching for Him. He knew that eventually I would get to the end of myself, because nothing and no one could satisfy that huge void in my heart, "but Jesus." You may want to pray with me: "How I love You, my Savior and my Lord, and I thank You that You judged my heart, not my superficiality! You alone counted me worthy to be saved!"

Verses to Meditate on and Memorize from Chapter 6

> ➤ Ecclesiastes 3:1-8 (NKJV): *To everything there is a season, a time for every purpose under heaven: A time to be born, and a time to die; a time to plant, and a time to pluck what is planted; a time to kill, and a time to heal; a time to break down, and a time to build up; a time to weep, and a time to laugh; a time to mourn, and a time to dance; a time to cast away stones, and a time to gather stones; a time to embrace, and a time to refrain from embracing; a time to gain, and a time to lose; a time to keep, and a time to throw away; a time to tear, and a time to sew; a time to keep silence, and a time to speak a time to love, and a time to hate; time of war, and a time of peace.*

> ➤ Jonah 2:2 (GNT): *In my distress, O Lord, I called to you, and you answered me. From deep in the world of the dead I cried for help, and you heard me.*

Journal your thoughts:

_____
_____
_____
_____
_____
_____
_____
_____
_____
_____
_____
_____

Journal your prayer:

_____
_____
_____
_____
_____
_____
_____
_____
_____
_____
_____
_____

Chapter 7

The Man of My Dreams

Because God has made us for Himself, our hearts are restless until they rest in Him. –Saint Augustine of Hippo

Thus far I haven't mentioned the religious upbringing I had when growing up. It's appropriate to do that now.

My parents were born and raised in the Anglican faith and were married in the Anglican Church. After a period of time, they converted to Catholicism. My siblings and I were christened as babies and raised in the Catholic faith. When my siblings and I were old enough, we had to attend catechism classes every Saturday morning. We also had to take our first Holy Communion at the appropriate age and were all confirmed when we turned thirteen. As a family we attended church every Sunday without fail. There were no arguments. It was not negotiable. We were especially observant at Easter and Christmas and enjoyed all the traditions and ceremonies of these two special occasions.

My first marriage was solemnized in the Catholic Church, even though my husband wasn't Catholic. When our two daughters were born, we had them christened. When our eldest daughter turned eight, she took her first Holy Communion. All my siblings were also married in the Catholic Church and all their children were christened and raised in the Catholic Church as well.

As a family, we never read the Bible, but both my parents were staunch in their beliefs and we were taught to revere God and expected to conform when it came to religious practices. We wouldn't have dared to miss church over Easter; nor would we ever eat meat on Good Friday. Those rituals seemed boring and meaningless at the time, but as you will read later, those same religious practices were what God used to eventually draw me to Himself.

When my first husband and I separated and discussed divorce, my family was understandably shocked. It is a well-known fact that the Catholic Church does not believe in divorce. Just for the record, neither did I. It happened anyway. It is the Catholic Church's belief that if you do get divorced, you are no longer welcome or recognized as a member of the Church. If you are divorced, you are not allowed to partake in Holy Communion. Thus, when I got divorced, I felt pretty much like I had committed the unforgiveable sin, and I no longer felt as though I belonged as a member of the Catholic community of faith.

At that time, to my family's dismay (especially my father's), I decided to leave the Catholic faith and find a church where my children and I would feel more comfortable and be more accepted as a divorced family. I'm not necessarily speaking about any particular Catholic Church, rather from my position as a divorcée. I felt uncomfortable in any church at that stage. I also had a sense that God was angry with me and that there would be no redemption for me at the end of my life. That was really the enemy putting lies into my head, because I didn't even know what redemption meant! That was in 1989.

My children and I visited a few churches in the area, which turned out to be traumatic exercises. Finding a different church after only ever knowing the Catholic faith and its ways was not easy. After a time, we eventually found our spiritual home at the local Methodist Church, where the environment was accepting and they embraced us fully as a family. My children went to Sunday school there, took part in the Friday night youth group, and were both eventually confirmed in the Methodist church, together with several of their friends from school.

I, on the other hand, never participated in any way, and I wasn't interested in doing so. I was doing my duty as a parent—taking my children to church. I did attend church myself most Sunday mornings, but the services meant nothing to me at all. It was purely an obligation that I performed each week and it was done without any thought or meaning. I never understood anything, and all I really remember were the hymns that were sung, and that was only because some of them reminded me of the hymns I'd sung in the Catholic Church. Apart from that, I could have been an atheist for all it meant to me.

ALPHA AND OMEGA

However, all that changed in January 1999. I was sitting in church one Sunday morning reading the bulletin. I had probably read the bulletin more than a hundred times before. But, somehow, this time was different. My interest was piqued by a notice about the Alpha course and a new session was starting at the end of that month. An introductory dinner was to be held where the course would be explained in more detail and the invitation was extended to anyone who wished to attend and find out more about Christianity.

The notice maintained that no question was too difficult or trivial to be asked, and they would do their level best to answer them all. I decided to register for the course; and when the time came, I went to the introductory evening on my own. Most of the people there knew one another, as they had been in the previous course together and were at the dinner to give testimony of what the course had done for them. I took a seat at a table with three couples and listened to the opening message by the senior minister.

From the moment he began to talk, he had my full attention. I was riveted and intrigued by everything he said. He told us that the course had been designed by an Anglican priest in the UK and was being used throughout the world to bring the message of Christianity in a simple and understandable way. The course class met one night a week over ten weeks, and somewhere in between the ten weeks we would all gather at the church for what was called the "Holy Spirit weekend." I was so excited and couldn't wait for the following week to start the course.

I told a friend of mine about the course (let's call her Ann), and she said she would like to attend with me. She signed up, and every week we would go off to the Alpha course, which was held in the church hall. We enjoyed a delicious meal, watched a video, broke up into small groups with a leader, and discussed what we had heard on the video.

It was a non-threatening, interesting, and totally captivating environment. The topics we discussed covered everything from "Why Jesus Died" to "How to Read the Bible." I had never heard such fascinating subjects before; certainly not in any church I had attended. I just could not get enough of all this fascinating knowledge I was learning every week—nothing could keep me away.

Week after week, Ann and I would leave the church, drive to her house, and sit outside in the car talking about all that we'd heard at the course. Ann was a Christian already (which I only found out much later, not that I would have recognized that fact), and she had been one for many years. She knew all about the subjects that were being discussed, but she'd never heard of the Alpha course and was as excited as I was. Our individual enthusiasm and interest spurred each other on until we had exhausted the topics from beginning to end. We would talk, laugh, and cry until early hours of the morning.

When I would eventually make my way home, I would lie awake for hours thinking about everything I had seen and heard. I lived on adrenalin and very little sleep during that time. I was wide awake and on fire during the day and night, yet still able to put in a full day's work. Ann and I spent a lot of time together in those early days, and I loved the way she shared her life's experiences with me. I realize now that God had sent her to me as a mentor. I gained so much knowledge and understanding at that time, which was vital for my growth and sustainability. We were both on a high in those wonderful times of discovering who this awesome God was. And then the Holy Spirit weekend arrived.

THE REAL MAN OF MY DREAMS

The various groups from the course met at the church on Saturday morning. We had a long, exciting discussion. Our minister explained clearly to us who the Holy Spirit was, what His role was in the Trinity, and how fundamental it was for every believer to be filled with the Holy Spirit. Then we were all given the opportunity to receive Jesus into our hearts, which I did. It was a life-changing moment for me, and one I will never forget. I was also very grateful that Ann was with me, because after I'd given my life to Christ, it felt like an anti-climax. Even though I knew I had just made the best and most important decision of my life, I didn't *feel* any different.

However, once Ann and I started talking about what had just happened and what it all meant, I was overwhelmed with joy and gratitude. I knew I had just crossed over to a new beginning and my life would never be the same from that day forward!

At last I could say with all truth and conviction that I had found the "Man of my dreams" and that Man was Jesus Christ, who was now my Savior and Lord. I also met God the Father and realized that He loved me totally and completely, no matter what I had done. I don't think there are words to describe the feeling of acceptance and love. One thing I did know was that if God could accept someone like me—someone who had not only messed up, but messed up big time, and still love me unconditionally—then that Person deserved my life, my wholehearted devotion. And to the best of my ability, I have given and continue to give my life to the One who first loved me—Abba Father, Jesus my Savior, and the precious Holy Spirit.

From the moment of my rebirth I just couldn't get enough of God. I was 42 years of age. I'd missed out on so much of real life, and I desperately wanted to learn about this God who had given His very life for me. I wanted to start living the life Jesus died for me to have. A life of abundance everyone spoke about. A life of giving and growing in Christ. Ann was instrumental in the growth of my faith in those early days of my journey with God, and I can honestly say that without her at my side, I probably would have given up long before my life with Christ had even begun!

Becoming a Christian did not instantly change my life for the better. Things didn't immediately become right. In fact, just the opposite happened. The wonderful thing, however, is that God knew that, and He didn't want me to give up and go back to that useless life I'd been living. He had a wonderful plan for my life, and He wanted me to grow into that plan, so He graciously gave me Ann to keep me grounded and on track. My salvation happened in 1999, and in the beginning of 2000 my first test came.

MOVING FORWARD

I was unfairly dismissed from my company. I was devastated, as I really loved my company and it had been a huge part of my life for so long. There was a positive spin, however. In the process of trying to sort out my dispute with the company, I discovered that God truly does cause all things to work together for the good of those who love Him and are called according to His purpose for them (Romans 8:28).

Not only did God sort out the whole mess for me, I also won my case at the Council for Conciliation, Mediation and Arbitration (CCMA) with a really good settlement; and if that wasn't enough, God opened a door to another job that was even better than the first one. My new boss was a wonderful Christian man and my mentoring continued as I met a group of Christian women who walked (and are still walking) this amazing journey with me.

The group of women I met at my company were from a Christian organization called Campus Crusade for Christ South Africa (CCCSA). CCCSA has couples who are in full-time ministry in the workplace. The men minister to the male executives and the wives hold a lunchtime Bible study class for women once a week, which I was invited to attend. I loved those weekly Bible studies and what I learned there each week. I grew in leaps and bounds and never stopped yearning for more.

I learned how to minister in the marketplace. I learned evangelistic and leadership skills. I learned how to identify felt needs of women and how to counsel and mentor them. At the end of 2001, I was leading the Bible studies at lunchtime and was giving motivational talks to women at various functions at my company. God is truly amazing, and when He wants things done, He opens doors that no one can close (Revelation 3:7-8).

I loved my Lord. I loved my life. I loved my job. For the first time in my life, I was living a life of purpose.

"But God" Chapter 7

Until the time I gave my life to Christ, I'd been searching for love and acceptance in all the wrong places. At the same time, my heart was breaking and nothing was filling that void in my heart. I knew the emptiness and loneliness I felt could only be filled by something other than what I was currently experiencing. Surely there was more. All of a sudden it appeared that my "prayers" offered to an "UNKNOWN GOD" were not offered to an "UNKNOWN GOD" at all!

We may not know what we are doing at any given time, "But God" does, all the time; and His plans for us are perfect. Thank Him for His perfect timing that saved us.

Verses to Meditate on and Memorize from Chapter 7

> Jeremiah 1:4-10 (GNT): *The Lord said to me, "I chose you before I gave you life, and before you were born I selected you to be a prophet to the nations." I answered, "Sovereign Lord, I don't know how to speak; I am too young." But the Lord said to me, "Do not say that you are too young, but go to the people I send you to, and tell them everything I command you to say. Do not be afraid of them, for I will be with you to protect you. I, the Lord, have spoken!" Then the Lord reached out, touched my lips, and said to me, "Listen, I am giving you the words you must speak. Today I give you authority over nations and kingdoms to uproot and to pull down, to destroy and to overthrow, to build and to plant."*

> 2 Peter 3:9 (GNT): *The Lord is not slow to do what he has promised, as some think. Instead, he is patient with you, because he does not want anyone to be destroyed, but wants all to turn away from their sins.*

Journal your thoughts:

_____

_____

_____

_____

_____

_____

_____

_____

_____

_____

Journal your prayer:

_____

_____

_____

_____

_____

_____

_____

_____

_____

_____

_____

_____

Chapter 8

The Best Love Story
May Begin with Goodbye

Getting over a painful experience is much like crossing monkey bars. You have to let go at some point in order to move forward.
–C.S. Lewis

At the time I gave my life to the Lord, I was working for a large public company as personal secretary to the chairman of the group. I was also the professional minute-taker for all the group company meetings. The chairman was due for retirement and wanted to know that I would be looked after once he retired. He encouraged me to continue working for the group, but on a contract basis, which I did.

Kevin and I were still dating, and the relationship continued to be stormy and challenging. On March 20, 2000 (a Monday night before a public holiday), I went to a mission meeting that was being held at my church. A minister from another circuit had come to our church to oversee a mission's week. He started the mission on Thursday that week, and Monday was the final evening. I don't remember everything about the mission, but one thing I do remember is the minister inviting people to come forward to the altar for prayer. I remember kneeling at the altar, crying my heart out again over the mess I'd made of my life.

Some good came out of that time of repentance. I left the church with my spirit lifted and feeling clean and purged. It's such an old-fashioned word, but so appropriate for how I felt. Kevin was staying over at my house, as was our usual practice on a weekend or public holiday. That evening, however, was different for me. I just couldn't face doing the usual routine again. I felt that if I let Kevin stay over, I would not feel this cleanliness the next day.

I asked him not to stay over, which he didn't take kindly to, but he respected my wishes nonetheless. That night as I sat in bed thinking about what I'd heard at the mission and my life in general, I got on my knees to pray. I couldn't put my prayers into words, so I prayed according to Romans 8:26-30 from the Easy-to-Read Version of the Bible:

Also, the Spirit helps us. We are very weak, but the Spirit helps us with our weakness. We don't know how to pray as we should, but the Spirit himself speaks to God for us. He begs God for us, speaking to him with feelings too deep for words. God already knows our deepest thoughts. And he understands what the Spirit is saying, because the Spirit speaks for his people in the way that agrees with what God wants. We know that in everything God works for the good of those who love him. These are the people God chose, because that was his plan. God knew them before he made the world. And he decided that they would be like his Son. Then Jesus would be the firstborn of many brothers and sisters. God planned for them to be like his Son. He chose them and made them right with him. And after he made them right, he gave them his glory.

I fell asleep and slept soundly until morning. When I awoke, the first thing I thought about was my relationship with Kevin. I prayed about it, and afterward I knew that I had no alternative but to end the relationship once and for all. It wasn't fair to either of us, and I owed it to myself and to him to be honest about how I felt since becoming a Christian. We met the next day and I discussed my decision with him. He was disappointed, but relieved. He'd been watching me since I got saved and he was not ready for that kind of spiritual commitment. We broke off our relationship, but agreed to remain friends.

I'd like to rewind for the moment.

When I was unfairly dismissed and at home waiting for my CCMA case to come up, I had a lot of time on my hands and I spent most of it studying God's Word, the Bible. God began to show me, through books, tapes, and messages from various sources, knowledge on sexual immorality.

I read books, listened to tapes, and found scriptures like 2 Corinthians 6:14-18 (GW):

Stop forming inappropriate relationships with unbelievers. Can right and wrong be partners? Can light have anything in common with darkness? Can Christ agree with the devil? Can a believer share life with an unbeliever? Can God's temple contain false gods? Clearly, we are the temple of the living God. As God said, "I will live and walk among them. I will be their God, and they will be my people." The Lord says, "Get away from unbelievers. Separate yourselves from them. Have nothing to do with anything unclean. Then I will welcome you." The Lord Almighty says, "I will be your Father, and you will be my sons and daughters."

And 1 Corinthians 6:9-20 (GW):

Don't you know that wicked people won't inherit God's kingdom? Stop deceiving yourselves! People who continue to commit sexual sins, who worship false gods, those who commit adultery, homosexuals, or thieves, those who are greedy or drunk, who use abusive language, or who rob people will not inherit God's kingdom. That's what some of you were! But you have been washed and made holy, and you have received God's approval in the name of the Lord Jesus Christ and in the Spirit of our God.

Someone may say, "I'm allowed to do anything," but not everything is helpful. I'm allowed to do anything, but I won't allow anything to gain control over my life. Food is for the stomach, and the stomach is for food, but God will put an end to both of them. However, the body is not for sexual sin but for the Lord, and the Lord is for the body. God brought the Lord back to life, and by his power God will also bring us back to life.

Don't you realize that your bodies are parts of Christ's body? Should I take the parts of Christ's body and make them parts of a prostitute's body? That's unthinkable! Don't you realize that the person who unites himself with a prostitute becomes one body with her? God says, "The two will be one." However, the person who unites himself with the Lord becomes one spirit with him.

Stay away from sexual sins. Other sins that people commit don't affect their bodies the same way sexual sins do. People who sin sexually sin against their own bodies. Don't you know that your body is a temple that belongs to the Holy Spirit? The Holy Spirit, whom you received from God, lives in you. You don't belong to yourselves. You were bought for a price. So bring glory to God in the way you use your body.

Suddenly, people started giving me material on the full meaning of biblical marriages and families and the roles God had ordained for husbands and wives. I was beginning to learn that godly marriages and families were supposed to be different from secular marriages. I started learning about the eternal consequences of adultery, divorce, and pornography that were permeating Christian marriages and families in huge proportions. I had at one time in my life been part of that world, and I knew full well the disastrous consequences of participating in that wickedness.

At the same time, God lead me to ministries like Focus on the Family, Family Policy Institute, Family Life, and Proverbs 31 Ministries in the USA, to name a few. In fact, I wrote in my journal that one day I would lead a Proverbs 31 ministry and write many books—and that at a time when I didn't even know what Proverbs 31 meant! God really has a sense of humor. It was a great time of researching, reading, learning, growing—and I loved every minute. Although I'd learned so much about sexual immorality and I'd been delivered from my past immoral life, I didn't become a godly woman overnight. Unfortunately, that didn't happen. I was a W-I-P (Woman In Progress), and God still had a lot of work to do in me before I would be a vessel that He could use in the area of godly purity.

HEALING AND WHOLENESS

In January 2001, my parents were in transit after having sold their home far quicker than they expected. They needed a place to stay, so they moved in with me. I moved into the spare room and literally became a child again, as my parents took on the role of looking after me.

It wasn't anything that was planned, it just happened because of circumstances. My mom cooked and cleaned for me, made all the meals and my lunches for work. Our everyday routine began with my dad taking me to the bus stop where I would catch the company bus to work. It was all a bit surreal, and the beginning of my journey to healing and wholeness. The next nine months were difficult ones for me. I knew God wanted me to set myself apart unto Him. To be still and allow Him to heal my brokenness and restore me to wholeness.

It strikes me now the irony of that period of healing being nine months. The same duration as a pregnancy, waiting for the promise of new birth. It was also the first time in my adult life that I found myself really single. No dating. No marriage. No male relationships. That felt weird and uncomfortable, but very necessary at the time.

Before Kevin and I broke up, we joined a drama society called Edenvale Amateur Drama Society, and we were practicing for a play that would be presented at the end of June that year. I saw Kevin once a week at rehearsals. It was awkward. He was distant. Neither of us knew how to act (pardon the pun). Each week I would put on a mask, did what I had to do, and finally I was very happy when the play acting (pardon the pun again) came to an end. When the play ended, there was no reason to see Kevin again, and that's when I went into solitary confinement, so to speak, for the next nine months. I didn't go out and no one visited me. I was alone, but I was never lonely. The Great Physician was with me all the time, and He was doing a huge healing work in my heart and body. He was busy restoring my soul.

I really loved my Savior, and I wanted to be the whole woman He created me to be. I never realized how broken I was—this was not going to be an overnight transformation. I often woke up in the middle of the night and journaled stuff—thoughts, prayers, things that I believed God was saying to me. I still have all those journals; and when I look at them today, I don't even recognize that person, that broken woman rising from the ashes.

At that time, I began to have strange dreams. I would wake up and remember the dream clearly and I would journal it so that I would not forget. I believe now that all these things were working together for my wholeness. Psalm 139 became my lifeline. I also received much emotional healing from reading a book called *Inner Healing*, by Betty Tapscott. I cried a lot and I cried often. It was just as well that my folks were living with me, for I might have done something extreme. I was that broken.

In May of that year I attended a New Life in the Spirit Seminar (LSS). This took me to a level deeper with the Lord and with my healing. LSS is a ten-week seminar on being baptized in the Holy Spirit. Each evening would begin with a time of praise and worship. Thereafter, we broke up into small groups to discuss a passage of Scripture on God's love (from a booklet we read during the week). Then we would have a small group discussion on what that Scripture passage meant to us personally.

At the end of the ten weeks, we were given the opportunity to be baptized in the Holy Spirit and to receive the gift of tongues, which I did. (Although let me clarify that I was already filled with the Holy Spirit on the day of my salvation and received the gift of tongues shortly after). To this day, that night remains embedded in my memory as the ultimate experience of the Holy Spirit like no other experience I have ever had before or since. It was incredible. Emotions I never knew I had surfaced from the depths of my soul and came out of my mouth in words that cannot be described or understood by the human mind.

When I finally got into bed that night, I couldn't sleep. I drifted into a sort of spiritual slumber. The following morning at 5 a.m. I woke up, and while I was worshipping and praising the Lord, suddenly I had a vision of Jesus standing at the bottom of the bed in the hospital room where my mom was giving birth to me. The moment I was born, Jesus took me in His arms, and holding me, looked into my eyes and said, "I've been waiting for you, because I knew the day you'd be born." Wow, talk about being loved and planned! That memory still has the power to bring me to tears! I am so loved and so blessed. Thank You, Jesus!

"But God" Chapter 8

Often when we hold on to things, be they good or bad, they are usually the very things that prevent us from receiving from God. We think we know better than God what is best for us, and we don't trust God to help us. We like what is familiar. We like our comfort zone; even when our comfort zone is not good for us. We prefer our routine and rut to God's redemption and reign in our lives.

We say we trust Him, but do we really? That was my biggest problem. I thought I trusted God, but clearly I didn't, because I didn't want to let go of my familiar, my comfort zone, or my routine and rut. That is what Kevin and my relationship was. It was comfortable and it was something we both knew. If one of us wanted out, it wasn't the end of the world, because we both knew that before long we would be back in that vicious cycle of co-dependency.

"But God" was not about to let me continue hurting myself any longer. He knew my weaknesses; and although He was patient with me, He would not let me stay in my familiar when He had so much more for me.

I once received an email story that went something like this:

A mother bought her little daughter a set of fake pearls. She was delighted and loved the pearls dearly. Her daddy realized she loved them so he decided to buy her a real set of pearls. The condition, however, was that she would have to give him her fake pearls without knowing that he would give her the real set in return. But she really, really did not want to give up her precious pearls.

She offered him everything from her doll to her coat and then some, but not her pearls. He was patient and loving, gentle and kind, and never pushed her into anything she did not want to do willingly. Eventually one day he asked her the question again:

"Sweetheart," he said, "are you ready to give Daddy your pearls?" This time, she very slowly, very tearfully, very reluctantly opened her hand and gave him her precious pearls. Immediately, he gave her the real ones in return, which were far more beautiful and precious than her fake ones. She squealed in delight and said, "Daddy, I've never seen anything so beautiful. Thank you so much!"

Is that a real story? I don't know, but I do know that it's a good illustration of what God has for us. His love is the real deal. If we would only learn to trust Him, He will do the rest. He's faithful even when we are unfaithful. The best love story really does begin with goodbye. Goodbye to everything in our lives that should not be there.

Verses to Meditate on and Memorize from Chapter 8

➤ Hebrews 12:1: *Therefore, since we are surrounded by such a huge crowd of witnesses to the life of faith, let us strip off every weight that slows us down, especially the sin that so easily trips us up. And let us run with endurance the race God has set before us.*

➤ Proverbs 3:5-6 (NKJV): *Trust in the Lord with all your heart, and lean not on your own understanding; in all your ways acknowledge Him, and He shall direct your paths.*

Journal your thoughts:

_____
_____
_____
_____
_____
_____
_____
_____
_____
_____

Journal your prayer:

_____

_____

_____

_____

_____

_____

_____

_____

_____

_____

_____

_____

_____

ENDNOTE

1. Many have found wisdom and comfort from these orga-
   nizations: Focus on the Family, www.focusonthefamily.
   com; www.safamily.co.za; Family Policy Institute, fam-
   ilypolicyinstitute.com; Family Life, www.familylife.org;
   www.mercyministry.com; and Proverbs 31 Ministries in
   the USA, www.proverbs31.org.

Chapter 9

A Heavenly Match

Marriages may be made in heaven, but man is responsible for the maintenance work. —Bertrand Russell

In August of the year that God healed me, my parents moved out of my home and into a retirement village, which would become their permanent home until my mother passed away in February 2016. It was a strange feeling having the place to myself again, and I began to settle back into a normal routine. At the end of September, one of my daughter's school friends sent me an invitation to her 21st birthday party—it was addressed to Kevin and me.

I had not seen or heard from Kevin since the play had ended months previously. I prayed about whether I should tell him about the invitation and ask him if he wanted to go with me. Before I could do that, he phoned me that week to invite me to mutual friend's home for a braai (barbeque). I hadn't been out for so long and I wasn't sure that it was the right thing to do, but I accepted anyway. He fetched me the following Saturday, and we had a lovely afternoon with old friends, who by the way were secretly hoping that we'd get back together again.

While we were together at our friend's house, I took the opportunity to ask him if he wanted to accompany me to Jenna's 21st party (not her real name) and he accepted with pleasure. A few weeks went by and the evening arrived. It was a dress-up affair, and I chose a long red dress to wear. I felt like a teenager going out on my first date. When he arrived, he looked very handsome in his suit and black tie. We had a lovely evening together and talked about many things. He said he missed me and asked me if I would consider giving our relationship another try.

I told him that I had been through a tough few months, and at that stage I didn't think the timing was right, but promised to pray about it.

"There She Goes Again"

At the end of the evening, Kevin took me home and I invited him inside for coffee. After we had coffee, he got up to go, and at that moment I thought to myself that I would love to spend the night with him again. I didn't think that one night together would hurt anyone. So, I asked him to stay the night, and my intentions were quite clear.

Fortunately, although I didn't think so at the time, he chose to be a gentleman and said, "No thank you." He pointed out that I had been the one to set the boundaries, and he was going to stick to them—even if I didn't want to! Well, to tell you the truth, I was quite peeved, and I went to bed feeling decidedly put out that he had rejected my advances.

Note: It has been my experience that whenever there has been a spiritual breakthrough, deliverance, or blessing in your life, satan will bring temptation into the situation.

The next day I woke up at 5 a.m. and sat bolt upright in bed. The events of the previous night came rushing back to my mind in vivid technicolor. I immediately got on my knees and said to the Lord, with a heart full of gratitude: "Thank You. Thank You. Thank You. Thank You. Thank You. Thank You, Lord, for protecting me last night!"

What I had done, or should I say what I had nearly *undone*, hit me like a ton of bricks when I woke up that morning. I nearly gave up months of healing and deliverance for the sake of one night of pleasure; I am eternally grateful to God for His divine intervention. When I speak at women's meetings and relate this story, I usually say the angels probably groaned: "Oh no, there she goes again, we've got our jobs cut out for us tonight"—and we all have a laugh. I can laugh about it now, but at the time it was not funny. It could have been a whole different picture the next morning. I am still grateful to Kevin that he chose to be a gentleman that night, to honor my commitment, even when I didn't want to!

Turning Point Times Two

That was a turning point in my relationship with Kevin, and I began praying fervently that he would accept Jesus as his Savior. We saw each other on and off over the next few months, but there was no commitment from either of us. I had taken what God had showed me months previously about being unequally yoked and about remaining pure until marriage seriously. I wanted to do the right thing, and more importantly the "God-thing," for the first time in my life. The months passed, and we both felt the pressure to be together. I was determined, however, not to give in to the temptation, not to buckle under that pressure.

One night when Kevin was visiting, I decided to ask him if he had ever thought of giving his life to Christ. I showed him the little red book "Why Jesus" (an Alpha resource), and asked him if he would like to read it. I told him if he had any questions we could talk about them. If he decided that he wanted to take this step of surrendering his life to Christ, which I pointed out had to be his decision and not be swayed by my faith, as this would be the most important decision he would ever make in his life, then I would do whatever I could to help him.

A week later, on February 14, 2002, he phoned me and said he wanted to make dinner for us at his house for Valentine's Day. I went over to his house, and after dinner he told me that he had read the book and decided that he wanted to accept Jesus as his Savior. I was overjoyed that he wanted to take this important step, and I prayed the sinner's prayer with him. A couple of months after that night, he decided to do the Alpha course at our church, which he enjoyed and it helped him understand in more depth about this new relationship with Jesus and what he could expect now that he was born again.

Kevin and I had discussed marriage, but not at any great length. However, one lazy Sunday afternoon when we were relaxing on the couch not doing anything of significance, out of the blue the subject of getting married came up and we began talking about a "Nike wedding"—in other words we said, "Let's just do it!" So, without any official "will you be my wife" proposal, we went right into planning our wedding and announced it to all our family and friends the very next day.

I was so excited. I knew this time it would be different. I was a godly woman and I'd learned so much about how to be a godly wife. I even promised God that because I loved Him so much I would be a "Wife after His own heart." I learned many years later that making that kind of promise to God (well, any promise to God), was very costly and not a good thing to do. We don't know what lies ahead of us—only God does.

We decided to get married on June 29 at our local church. In no time at all, the church and minister were booked. The venue and caterers hired. A draft invitation sent to the printers. Honeymoon booked and paid for, and our first night together as husband and wife secretly booked and paid for by me, as a gift to my husband-to-be. There was great excitement and a hive of activity for weeks. No one was at all surprised at our decision to get married. In fact, everyone was delighted that we had finally decided to make it official, as we had been dating for long enough, as far as they were concerned. We agreed.

BIBLICAL MARRIAGE PREPARATION

A month before the wedding, my friend at CCCSA sent us an invitation to Bruce Wilkinson's marriage course, "A Biblical Portrait of Marriage." We signed up and spent the weekend learning fundamental truths on marriage preparation and what God expected from us as a godly couple. It was an excellent course, and one of the best courses I have ever attended on marriage and marriage preparation. We received much good, sound, biblical advice, as we prepared to take that giant step of marriage.

I felt even more confident after we had completed the course that I was eventually going to get this marriage and godly-wife thing right and be able to testify of how it should be done. Rah! Rah! Rah! What does the Bible say about pride? "Pride goes before destruction, and haughtiness before a fall" (Proverbs 16:18 NLT). I sure learned that the hard way.

At last the day I had been waiting for so long arrived. I woke early and spent some quiet time with the Lord, thanking Him for everything He had done for me and for bringing me to that point in my life.

I also thanked Him for allowing me to do marriage again—His way. Because of His grace in my and Kevin's lives, we were given a second chance at marriage. God is truly a God of second chances. I felt like a princess about to marry her prince charming, and I was looking forward to doing life with Kevin "till death do us part."

The day was perfect. It was a chilly winter's day with the promise of winter warmth later. Both my sisters (my younger sister had flown in from Australia), and both my daughters were with me (my girls were my bridesmaids). Together we did our makeup and hair and got in each other's way as five women managed to get all dressed up in a very small space. I had already packed everything for our special night together that I had booked and kept secret. I sent a text message to my future husband telling him how much I loved him and how much I was looking forward to being his wife. Then I was ready to go to the church and walk down the aisle where my beloved was waiting for me.

The only unfortunate incident, in an otherwise perfect day, was that the hairdresser was very late, which made us late getting to the church. Finally, however, everything was sorted out and I made my grand appearance—about thirty minutes late! We chose the song, "From This Moment" (by Shania Twain) to be played in the church and for our first dance later that day. We chose Psalm 127:1 (NKJV) for our wedding message, "Unless the Lord builds the house, they labor in vain who build it; unless the Lord guards the city, the watchman stays awake in vain."

And the minister also included in his message Ecclesiastes 4:9-12 (GNT):

Two are better off than one, because together they can work more effectively. If one of them falls down, the other can help him up. But if someone is alone and falls, it's just too bad, because there is no one to help him. If it is cold, two can sleep together and stay warm, but how can you keep warm by yourself. Two people can resist an attack that would defeat one person alone. A rope made of three cords is hard to break.

As far as I was concerned, God had brought us together. He was the center of our lives and He would be the head of our marriage, so nothing could go wrong—right? I was blissfully unaware of how much could go wrong as I entered into marriage that day with heavenly expectations for the third time in my life.

Every part of our day was perfect and we both enjoyed it tremendously. We especially couldn't wait to get away to celebrate our first night as husband and wife. We had waited sixteen months in total, and I knew it was going to be well worth the wait!

Three days after the wedding day excitement had subsided and we had moved into our new home, we left for our two-week honeymoon to George in the Western Cape. We enjoyed exploring a part of South Africa that was totally new to both of us. The beauty of the mountains and the sea was breathtaking, and God's creation came alive as we discovered and visited places we had only ever heard of until that time.

After we explored George, Knysna, Mossel Bay, Plettenberg Bay (which later became our home, but more about that in a later chapter), Oudtshoorn, and Graaff Reinet, we made our way back to Johannesburg to our home, which we had purchased together and was in the process of being registered in our names. We were about to begin our idyllic life as husband and wife for the second time for Kevin and the third time for me.

Life was good!

"BUT GOD" CHAPTER 9

Why do people get married? If you Google that question, you'll come up with 312 million answers! Some of them would make your hair stand on end, but I believe marriage is a God-given desire to folk like us who want to be married God's way. (Although there is only one way to be married and that *is* God's way).

It is the reason why Kevin and I wanted to be married. We purposely chose Psalm 127:1 for our marriage verse, as neither of us had the Lord in our lives when we were married previously. It was of utmost importance to us that this time around God would not only be in our lives, but He would be the Head of our home. It is also why I titled this chapter A Heavenly Match and included Ecclesiastes 4:9-12. However, none of these facts would guarantee a "happy ever after" or a "until death do us part" life, as much as we wanted that. We are imperfect people who live in a sin-sick world. Let's face it, becoming one with someone who does not always share your views, is not going to be easy.

"But God" is for marriage, not against it; and with His grace in our lives, we are more able to take on the challenge of becoming one as husband and wife and living together under one roof than if we didn't have God in our lives. But it does take time and effort.

Verses to Meditate on and Memorize from Chapter 9

Genesis 2:18-25: *Then the Lord God said, "It is not good for the man to be alone. I will make a helper who is just right for him." So the Lord God formed from the ground all the wild animals and all the birds of the sky. He brought them to the man to see what he would call them, and the man chose a name for each one. He gave names to all the livestock, all the birds of the sky, and all the wild animals. But still there was no helper just right for him. So the Lord God caused the man to fall into a deep sleep. While the man slept, the Lord God took out one of the man's ribs and closed up the opening. Then the Lord God made a woman from the rib, and he brought her to the man. "At last!" the man exclaimed. "This one is bone from my bone, and flesh from my flesh! She will be called 'woman,' because she was taken from 'man.'" This explains why a man leaves his father and mother and is joined to his wife, and the two are united into one. Now the man and his wife were both naked, but they felt no shame.*

Journal your thoughts:

_____

_____

_____

_____

_____

_____

_____

_____

_____

_____

Journal your prayer:

_____

_____

_____

_____

_____

_____

_____

_____

_____

_____

_____

_____

Chapter 10

A Wife After God's Own Heart

God-confidence comes as the Holy Spirit works in us. As we pray and when we make choices that honor God, the Holy Spirit fills us with His power for ministry. When we are filled with God's goodness, we are confidently and effectively able to share His love and joy. As women of prayer open to the transforming touch of the Holy Spirit, we will find His divine life in us overflowing into the lives of others. –Elizabeth George from her book, *A Woman After God's Own Heart*

We were married precisely two months when we had our first awful fight. The detail is not important, but I was devastated that it was so soon into our married life. What happened to all those promises and vows we made? I prayed a lot and asked God to forgive me for being the one to cause the argument in the first place. We talked it through, apologized to one another and got back on track.

Through that unpleasant incident, I learned that my husband did not take kindly to dragging arguments out. His way was, sort it out, move on, and don't bring it up again. I remember reading a joke where two men were talking about an argument one of them had with his wife and he said it was because she always got so historical. The other guy said, "Don't you mean hysterical?" The other guy said, "No, I mean historical. She always brings up everything from the past!" I learned not to do that.

Instead, I learned to stuff things away. I learned to keep the peace, be the peacemaker, walk on eggshells a lot of the time, and generally to toe the line. However, I was never very good at any of that, and neither was my husband. So there were days when I dug my heels in and so did he.

Most of the time, however, I'd be the one to give in, mainly because of the promise I'd made to God to be a wife after His own heart. I didn't do it with a good heart though, so as a result, guilt and condemnation were close companions of mine in those days.

By June the following year, before our first anniversary, because of a lack of communicating the way we'd been taught at the marriage prep course, our home was filled with tension and conflict. I got to the stage where I decided to move out and stay at a friend's place for a while to sort out my feelings. Kevin was devastated that I would take such a drastic step. So was I. Nevertheless, I felt that I needed some time away to digest what was happening in this marriage that I'd held out such high hopes for.

After a week of mulling through the first year of our marriage and speaking to God about it all, I decided that being separated wasn't the answer and I needed to go back to my marriage and work things out God's way. I didn't understand why we couldn't work things out, particularly as God was on our side. We got back together again, promising each other that things would be different from then on. That we would both try to do things God's way and not think of ourselves, but of one another.

For my birthday that year, my daughter gave me the book *A Woman After God's Own Heart* by Elizabeth George. Even though I felt as far as the East is from the West from being a woman after God's own heart, I was determined to be one—if it was the last thing I did! After all, there must have been something I was doing right for my daughter to have penned these words:

"Dearest Mom, Hope you enjoy reading this book. When I saw this book, the first person I thought of was you! Love always, S"

How could I not try my utmost to make my marriage work after such beautiful and meaningful words? So Kevin and I purchased marriage devotionals. We enlisted the help of godly married friends who seemed to have passed through the stage we were in and were able to counsel us. I even volunteered to be a speaker on the marriage prep course at our church, and ironically the subject I spoke on was communication!

At the beginning of 2004, I heard about "The Marriage Course" by Nicky and Sila Lee from Holy Trinity Church in Brompton. I persuaded Kevin to attend, and he agreed.

The Marriage Course is hosted by Nicky and Sila Lee who are co-authors of *The Marriage Book*. They have been married for more than 30 years. The evenings are designed for any married couple wishing to build a strong and lasting relationship.

Topics covered include:
> Building Strong Foundations
> The Art of Communication
> Resolving Conflict
> The Power of Forgiveness
> The Impact of Family - Past and Present
> Good Sex
> Love in Action

Each couple's privacy is respected as there is no group discussion and no requirement to disclose anything about their relationship to anyone else. The course, while based on Christian principles, is very helpful for any couple with or without a Christian faith or church background. Visit: http://www.htb.org.uk/marriage.

The concept of The Marriage Course is wonderful, and the content is relevant, valid, and beneficial. However, like every course, if you don't follow it through and apply what you learn to the situation, you've wasted your time and money, and no benefit will be gained. The course facilitators place a huge emphasis (and rightly so) on creating *marriage time* in your diary once a week. Not only for the homework (which is essential), but also for the couple to spend time together. It might be the only time you get to do that.

The Marriage Course evenings are designed to create an atmosphere of intimacy between you and your spouse. With a simple meal at a table for two, watching a video on the topic for the evening's lesson as a group, and then back to your table to discuss the questions in the book.

The first week found us sitting down together like two good little students and discussing the homework and getting through it without too much disagreement—after all, we couldn't go too wrong with a topic entitled "Building Strong Foundations." We were pretty pleased with ourselves that we managed to get through that first week successfully.

The second week was a different story altogether; instead of learning "The Art of Communicating," we learned the art of how *not* to communicate after learning The Art of Communicating!

Followed by the third week's topic "Resolving Conflict," which we desperately needed but turned into "Unresolved Conflict!"

By the fourth week we really had to sit down and take that week's topic to heart: "The Power of Forgiveness." We both agreed that forgiveness was necessary, and once we discussed our disagreements and had forgiven one another, peace filled our home once again and we were able to move past the conflict and focus on what God wanted to do in both of us through the course.

At the end of the course, we went over the checklist that is discussed in the final chapter. The checklist is to ensure the participants stay on track; and if you stray for whatever reason, you can go back to the manual and do the exercises again until that particular hurdle is jumped successfully. It really is an excellent course and well worth the time, money, and effort to do it.

GOALS

Before we were married, one of the things we discussed was our ministry goals. At that time, I discussed with Kevin that one day in the future my heart's desire was to go into full-time ministry. I wasn't exactly sure what the ministry would look like, except I was sure it would include marriage, family, and women and that I would speak, write, and teach on those subjects.

In October 2003, I wrote in my journal that God laid on my heart that one day I would write a women's daily devotional. I didn't state when or how that would happen. I do remember thinking at the time that I had to have been mistaken in thinking that God would allow someone like me to speak into other women's lives. I couldn't get my own life right, how was I ever going to help other women. However, the passion and the vision wouldn't go away, and the more I thought about it, the more unlikely it seemed—but at the same time, the more passionate I became.

In 2004 I also began my speaking ministry. Not that I knew it was a speaking ministry then. Looking back, I can see how God was already training me for what was to come. I also wrote in my journal that God had laid on my heart that the daily devotional would be for married women, and I would start a women's Bible study, prayer, and share group. I felt privileged and excited, but I wanted to know the how, what, where, and when. I was ill-equipped on every level to take on a project of this size, but I also knew that if it was a "God-thing," He would be the one to lead and guide me.

At the beginning of 2004, I was invited to give my testimony at one of the morning services at our church. I was nervous and excited at the same time to be sharing my testimony of how God had changed my life with His amazing unconditional love and grace. Shortly after that, one of the senior ministers at our church resigned and I was asked to give a farewell speech to him and his family. Again I was a bundle of nerves, but the speech flowed and it was with a joyful heart that I could deliver that message to him and his family.

Sometimes when I reflect on that time in my life, I wonder if I messed things up by running ahead of God. But then I encourage myself with stories from the Bible like Job's story or Joseph's life story and see how God worked in their lives. After reading these stories, I arrive at the conclusion (and it's my own personal view), that no matter what's happening in our lives, if our desire is to please God and our hearts are sincere in following Him to the best of our ability and understanding, we cannot be out of His will and He will cause all things to work together for good to those who love Him and have been called according to *His* purpose for us, as He promises in Romans 8:28 (GNT):

> *We know that in all things God works for good with those who love him, those whom he has called according to his purpose.*

"But God" Chapter 10

My heart's desire since being saved has been to be a woman after God's own heart. When I began praying for Kevin to accept Christ as his Savior and he did, one of the verses I prayed is found in Genesis 2:18 (GW): "Then the Lord God said, 'It is not good for the man to be alone. I will make a helper who is just right for him.'"

I said, "God, it's not good that Kevin is alone, he needs me as his helper." And then I did a really foolish thing—I promised God that if He would save Kevin and bring us together in marriage, I would be a wife after His own heart! As I mentioned previously, it's unwise to promise God anything. "But God" thankfully knew that my promise to Him was coming from a sincere and clean heart. That I really believed I could fulfill that promise, especially with God on my side.

The truth is, I could no more change Kevin than fly to the moon. That promise was therefore futile, and all I ended up doing was living a frustrated, unfulfilled life.

"But God" is faithful. He always keeps His promises, and He kept His promise to me, even when I couldn't keep my promise to Him. God's grace covers a multitude of sins. The New Living Translation of the Bible's dictionary-concordance definition of a promise is "to covenant, pledge, or give assurance."

One last piece of advice: marriage is a ministry and a calling; and as such, we serve God first and foremost, then we serve one another—we need God to do the latter!

Verses to Meditate on and Memorize from Chapter 10

➤ Ephesians 5:21-33 Spirit-Guided Relationships: Wives and Husbands: *And further, submit to one another out of reverence for Christ. For wives, this means submit to your husbands as to the Lord. For a husband is the head of his wife as Christ is the head of the church. He is the Savior of his body, the church. As the church submits to Christ, so you wives should submit to your husbands in everything.*

For husbands, this means love your wives, just as Christ loved the church. He gave up his life for her to make her holy and clean, washed by the cleansing of God's word. He did this to present her to himself as a glorious church without a spot or wrinkle or any other blemish. Instead, she will be holy and without fault. In the same way, husbands ought to love their wives as they love their own bodies. For a man who loves his wife actually shows love for himself. No one hates his own body but feeds and cares for it, just as Christ cares for the church. And we are members of his body.

As the Scriptures say, "A man leaves his father and mother and is joined to his wife, and the two are united into one." This is a great mystery, but it is an illustration of the way Christ and the church are one. So again I say, each man must love his wife as he loves himself, and the wife must respect her husband.

Journal your thoughts:

_____

_____

_____

_____

_____

_____

_____

_____

_____

_____

_____

_____

_____

_____

_____

_____

_____

_____

Journal your prayer:

_____

_____

_____

_____

_____

_____

_____

_____

_____

_____

_____

_____

_____

_____

_____

_____

Chapter 11

I Don't Wanna Play House

The thing I have discovered about working with personal finance is that the good news is that it is not rocket science. Personal finance is about 80 percent behavior. It is only about 20 percent head knowledge. I believe that through knowledge and discipline, financial peace is possible for all of us. –Dave Ramsey

"I don't wanna play house, I know it can be fun. I've watched mommy and daddy and if that's the way it's done, I don't wanna play house, it makes my mommy cry, 'cause when she plays house, my daddy says goodbye." You may recognize those lyrics from a song produced and sung by South African singer Barbara Ray back in the 1970s. I heard it a few years ago and used it as an introduction to a talk I gave on the subject of divorce. I used it to open this chapter because I was at a stage in our marriage where once again, I did not want to play house anymore:

> ➤ Even though we had gone through The Marriage Course and we both enjoyed it and gained a lot of knowledge

> ➤ Even though we felt better equipped to deal with the tough issues

> ➤ And even though we'd made promises to keep our marriage on track, one thing led to another and before we knew it, all our good intentions went out the window and things started to go wrong.

In no time at all we stepped out of our routine of having marriage time. Our lack of meaningful and effective communication and resolving conflict God's way ended in arguments, hot tempers, and angry words. All the good stuff we learned went out the window! Our arguments were mostly about finances and financial pressures.

We were given some lessons on financial management God's way in the past, but we hadn't made the effort we should have to apply those lessons to our lives.

FINANCE ISSUES

At this stage, I'd like to camp for a time on the subject of finances. Our less-than-satisfactory financial circumstances were some of the principal issues that caused most of the arguments in our marriage. The other issues were about the baggage we'd both brought into the marriage. Baggage that hadn't been dealt with and baggage that had been dealt with but still managed at times to creep into our lives and trip us up.

It has been said in jest that "When money goes out the window, love goes out the door." True? I'm not sure, but I do know that unstable finances in a marriage cause much distress between husbands and wives, and you're likely to do things that you probably wouldn't do if finances were stable.

When Kevin left school, he became an apprentice in electronics through the local Post and Telecommunications Company in Bulawayo. He continued in this trade for about three years after he had immigrated to South Africa. After three years, he was offered a partnership in a stationery and allied business, which he decided to pursue. When we met in 1994, he was still in that partnership and continued in the stationery and printing industry until 2006. At that time a friend spoke to Kevin about the possibility of changing careers into the real estate industry. They discussed this at length, and after some investigation, Kevin decided to terminate the partnership, leave the stationery business, and enter the real estate industry.

Before we go into his journey in the real estate industry, I need to say that I was working at that time as a personal assistant at the country's largest energy and gas supplier, and I was earning a good salary with good benefits. In the real estate business, Kevin was a commission-only earner, and it was a huge frustration for me. It was a constant battle to draft a monthly budget and juggle figures to meet that budget.

Kevin had lived for a long time on his own, thus he never saw the need to bother with a personal budget, especially as he didn't have family commitments *per se*. If he wanted to buy something, he bought it. If he wanted to be extravagant at times, he would be extravagant. And if he wanted to be "spendthrifty" at times, he would be. In other words, it was about him and not a family.

Whereas in my case, I'd been a single parent for many years and I had two daughters to think of. I had to educate, feed, clothe, indulge, and entertain them on one salary, and I put my children's needs first. I never learned how to budget or work with money when I was growing up and my mindset—wrong or right—was "live for today because tomorrow might never come." As a result, we never had extras for emergencies, and we lived from one payday to the next.

FINANCIAL FRUSTRATIONS

When I was married to my children's father, I handled the finances and what was his was mine and what was mine was mine! When Kevin and I were first married, it was a case of what was Kevin's was Kevin's and what was mine was ours! Jokes aside, the frustrations grew and we struggled to communicate with any success about finances. I stuffed away most of my frustrations. This was obviously not a good thing to do. Invariably the subject would come up at the most inappropriate time and manner, which caused terrible arguments that led to days of hurt, anger, and silence—and not golden silence!

This pattern continued month after month (sometimes week after week), year after year, and it was a subject that couldn't be raised without angry words being spoken by one or both of us. The more I tried to talk about it, the more he closed up and the more frustrated I became. During these times I tried prayer, fasting, counsel, studying the Word, and listening to tapes on finances God's way. When I was sure I learned enough to help us out of tough spots, I'd try again to talk about it with Kevin, only to be met with the same brick wall. Eventually, I gave up. So when our friend (who was also my prayer partner) suggested Kevin try real estate, I encouraged him to go for it, thinking that maybe this was the change needed to soften his heart and get our finances on track.

The agency Kevin worked for was owned by two Christian families. From day one Kevin took to real estate and seemed to be a born real estate agent, if there is such a thing. After he completed his board exam and began showing houses, he went from strength to strength and it looked as though he had at last found his niche. He sold houses one after the other and he was often recognized as "Agent of the Month." He also won an award for agent of the quarter and received a hi-tech sound system as his prize. Shortly after he won that award, one of the conveyancing companies that the agency dealt with, announced a competition for Agent of the Year, the prize being a trip for two to Mauritius, all expenses paid. Kevin is a competitive person and he was determined to become the winner of that competition. As the gala evening arrived where the winner would be announced, three finalists were chosen—Kevin was one of them.

The evening was a huge success. The food and décor were first class and the speeches and accolades were filled with humor and praise. Eventually the time arrived to announce the winner. The principal, let's call him Chris, asked the band for a drumroll, and then with silence and bated breath, the envelope was opened. Kevin was announced "Agent of the Year"! The whole company broke out in loud applause and Kevin was in his element.

I was so proud of him, and we were looking forward to enjoying a trip to Mauritius. It was a wonderful evening and the perfect ending to a really good year for Kevin. The time away was perfect. From the flight, to the hotel, to the food, to the sea, to the sunsets and sunrises, to the tours we enjoyed. We loved every part of it, and we thanked God for His amazing grace and favor as we sat on our balcony and watched the sunset over the sea the evening before we left.

FROM PERFECTION TO PROBLEMS

When we returned home from Mauritius, things were not as good as when we left eight short days before. There were rumors that one of the principals wanted out. Many changes were being made, and tension and conflict among management and agents were brewing. Some agents were asked to leave, as they were not pulling their weight. Others left of their own accord, disillusioned with the real estate market. In the month of June prior to our trip to Mauritius, the new Credit Act had been promulgated and banks were not giving home loans as easily as in the past. This made the real estate agent's job really difficult. Kevin started looking at changing agencies. I wasn't sure if that was the right move to make at that time, but that was his call to make. Was it better to be in a situation where you knew the market, or was it better to try another agency? The answer didn't come easily.

In the same year that Kevin won the award, our younger daughter was married in Plettenberg Bay. Family and friends flew there for the wedding and it gave us an opportunity to explore that part of the world. Even though we'd honeymooned in that area, we hadn't really explored Plettenberg Bay at the time. We both loved Plettenberg Bay and jokingly (or maybe not) we both said that we could easily live in Plettenberg Bay, given the right circumstances.

While Kevin was investigating other agencies, he came across an advertisement that the same agency he was working for in Johannesburg had recently opened a franchise in Plettenberg Bay and plans of moving there began to form in his mind. He discussed it with me and we prayed about it. He began communicating with the franchisor in Plettenberg Bay, and she encouraged Kevin to seriously consider joining them.

It was more of a huge move for me than it was for Kevin. For me it meant leaving my daughters, grandchildren, and parents behind, which I wasn't sure I wanted to do. One of the reasons I was unsure about the move was that a series of tragedies had struck our family from 2006 to 2008, and those tragedies weighed heavily on my heart as we considered the move. Eventually, Kevin made up his mind that he wanted to make the move, and as his wife I felt I had to support him in that decision. He pointed out that Johannesburg was just a flight away and I could visit the family as often as I wanted to.

In reality, it didn't really work that way. With the decision finalized, we began to make our plans to relocate to a new province and a totally different way of life—about 800 miles away.

"BUT GOD" CHAPTER 11

Various articles I have read over the years have stated that financial woes do not cause couples to divorce. In fact, couples actually put off getting divorced, because they can't afford it. There are many reasons why couples decide to divorce, but to decide not to divorce because they don't have the money is just sad and delaying the inevitable. I do, however, understand why a statement like that would be made and I can assure you that even though those couples may not get divorced because they can't afford to, it doesn't change the fact that every waking moment, they want to!

Financial lack and insurmountable debt are horrible. They consume ones' thoughts and sometimes immobilize couples to do anything about it, as they don't know which way to turn. There seems to be no way out. Having said all this, I've been told by some people who do have money and made all the right financial decisions, that they are no happier than those with financial problems. They are just more comfortable in their misery, whatever that means! That's also a sad statement to make.

"But God" came through for us even when we were in dire straits. He provided in the most unexpected ways, and we must honestly say that we have never gone without a roof over our heads, a meal on the table, or without a friend by our side sharing our burdens. And if the truth be told, our financial woes were mainly due to what we had sown. Sowing and reaping is a law that comes to pass for the good or bad. We had to learn to sow for the good, which was a hard lesson, but one worth mastering. We both thank God for His faithfulness once again.

Verses to Meditate on and Memorize from Chapter 11

> Galatians 6:7 (GW): *Make no mistake about this: You can never make a fool out of God. Whatever you plant is what you'll harvest.*

Law of Sowing and Reaping

When God tells us that we will reap what we sow, He is not punishing us; He's telling us how things really are.

Sometimes we don't reap what we sow because someone steps in and reaps the consequences for us. For example, like children who wait until the last minute to do their school projects, and the parents end up taking over. What are the children learning? Teens and young adults who call parents to bail them out—what are they learning?

Just as we can interfere with the law of gravity by catching a glass tumbling off the table, people can interfere with the Law of Cause and Effect by stepping in and rescuing irresponsible people. Rescuing people from the natural consequences of their choices enables them to continue in irresponsible behavior.

Establishing boundaries helps people stop interrupting the Law of Sowing and Reaping. Boundaries force people who are sowing to also do the reaping. Just confronting doesn't help. Telling them what we think about their behavior and that they need to change is only NAGGING. They don't feel the need to change because their behavior is not causing them any pain. **Confronting irresponsible people is not painful to them; only consequences are.**

If a person is wise, confronting the person may change the behavior. But people caught in destructive patterns are usually not wise. They need to suffer consequences before they change their behavior. The Bible tells us it is worthless to confront foolish people: "Do not rebuke a mocker or he will hate you; rebuke a wise man and he will love you" (Proverbs 9:8). (https://bible.org/seriespage/consequences-law-sowing-and-reaping-lesson-2-6)

Journal your thoughts:

_____

_____

_____

_____

_____

_____

_____

_____
_____
_____
_____
_____
_____
_____
_____
_____
_____

Journal your prayer:

_____
_____
_____
_____
_____
_____
_____
_____
_____
_____
_____
_____
_____
_____
_____
_____
_____

Chapter 12

Laying the Foundation

Therefore everyone who hears these words of Mine and acts on them is like a wise man who built his house on the rock. The rain fell, the torrents raged and the winds blew and beat against that house; yet it did not fall, because its foundation was on the rock.
–Matthew 7:24-25 (Berean Study Bible)

I was blessed in June 2005 to attend a speaking and writing training course through Proverbs 31 Ministries USA. It was an incredible time of learning and just generally spending time getting to know the women at the conference and enjoying a vacation too.

I was thoroughly exhausted by the time I returned to South Africa, and was feeling burnt out. After a week or two of being home, I emailed a friend I'd met at the conference and told her that I was feeling spiritually flat. I said that I was tired, irritable, and didn't know what to do next. I had all this information that I'd gained at the conference and loads of notes I had journaled during our many travels, but I wasn't sure what to do with it all, or where to start—and worse than that, I didn't know if I even wanted to! Thankfully, "B" is a woman who has lots of experience and she managed to speak to me with wise, sound counsel and said that I needed to get some sleep, get back into my routine as quickly as possible, and pray for God's guidance.

The following are her exact words from an email reply to my letter:

Oh, how good it is to hear from you! I wish right now I could give you a hug, your marching orders and a pep talk to "Go and preach the Gospel." My dear friend, I don't know what God has in store for you, for Kevin or for the women of South Africa. What I do know, however, is this. You are holy.

You are a dear, precious child of God. You are dearly loved. You are the apple of His eye, the salt and light of the earth, chosen and appointed to bear fruit, God's workmanship and a co-worker in His kingdom. Beyond that, Leonie, I don't know much else. But if you want, I will be your prayer warrior. I will come alongside you daily asking Jesus Christ to remember you. I will make your prayer requests known to the Proverbs 31 team. I will gather up other prayer warriors who will come boldly before His throne of grace on your behalf. If you are willing, Leonie, read Acts 26:16-18: "Now get up and stand on your feet. I have appeared to you to appoint you as a servant and as a witness of what you have seen and will see of me. I will rescue you from your own people and from the Gentiles. I am sending you to them to open their eyes and turn them from darkness to light, and from the power of Satan to God, so that they may receive forgiveness of sins and a place among those who are sanctified by faith in me."

If your heart cry is, "Holy LORD. What?" I will pray this passage with you daily asking our heavenly Father to give you the Spirit of wisdom and revelation so that you may know Him better and to open the eyes of your heart to know the hope to which He has called you. But, I will also caution you, Leonie. Watch out. For when God's children pray, earnestly and fervently, the LORD of the universe moves.

I am so glad to have finally met you in person, Leonie. I've already come to love your gentle voice, your calm spirit, your loving heart; and I look forward to others coming to know you too.

Your sister in Christ, B.

"BUT GOD" CHAPTER 12

My trip to the United States was truly a God-sent, God-ordained blessing. Before the trip, I didn't believe these types of blessings could happen to the likes of someone like me. I know differently now, and I will try not to limit God again in the future! What I found after attending this amazing conference was that it just whetted my appetite for more. I found myself unsettled and restless for more.

➤ More networking with other godly women.

➤ More information that catapults me into new areas of ministry.

➤ More meeting and mixing with different cultures.

➤ Just more.

Like the book I read, *Longing for More* by Ruth Hayley Barton, I too wanted more. "But God" wanted me in a place of quiet. A place where He could prepare my heart for the work He had prepared for me to do. So, for the next few years I lived between sitting at His feet and volunteering in various opportunities to minister to women. The problem with the ministering was that it left me frustrated and still longing for more. I had to learn to stop when He said stop and go when He said go. In other words, I had to stop running ahead of Him trying to do things in my own strength and learn to listen to His voice and not my own. It wasn't easy.

It's still not easy, but it's the only way. If God is not *the* foundation, we may as well give up now, because the work will never last. When the storms of life come—and they will come—our lives will crash and crumble. Little did I know the storms were coming!

Verses to Meditate on and Memorize from Chapter 12:

➤ Matthew 7:24-25 (GW) The Wise and Foolish Builders: *Therefore, everyone who hears what I say and obeys it will be like a wise person who built a house on rock. Rain poured, and floods came.*

Winds blew and beat against that house. But it did not collapse, because its foundation was on rock.

> Psalm 46:10: *"Be still, and know that I am God! I will be honored by every nation. I will be honored throughout the world."*

Journal your thoughts:

_____

_____

_____

_____

_____

_____

_____

_____

_____

Journal your prayer:

_____

_____

_____

_____

_____

_____

_____

_____

_____

Chapter 13

Ministry Beginnings

Ministry Beginnings—Family First. –Leonie Leo-Brewer

The email I received from B that day, September 5, 2005, gave me the motivation I needed to get back on my feet and to move into the work that God had called me to. From that day onward, I got back into my routine quiet times with the Lord and began to journal once again. About 12:30 on the morning of October 11, 2005, I woke up suddenly and couldn't get back to sleep. Eventually at 2 a.m., I got up and went into the spare room, where I usually spent my quiet times. I wrote the following:

> God has laid on my heart a plan to share Jesus with my family and friends. I believe God wanted me to:

- Have a Christmas family gathering.
- Invite all my family, including my in-laws and friends.
- Have the function at a church in Edenvale in November.
- Share my testimony, have Kevin share his testimony, and one other family member share their testimony.

The Scripture verses that came to my mind were: Luke 2:8-14: *"That night there were shepherds staying in the fields nearby, guarding their flocks of sheep. Suddenly, an angel of the Lord appeared among them, and the radiance of the Lord's glory surrounded them. They were terrified, but the angel reassured them. 'Don't be afraid!' he said. 'I bring you good news that will bring great joy to all people. The Savior—yes, the Messiah, the Lord—has been born today in Bethlehem, the city of David! And you will recognize him by this sign: You will find a baby wrapped snugly in strips of cloth, lying in a manger.' Suddenly, the angel was joined by a vast host of others—the armies of heaven—praising God and saying, 'Glory to God in highest heaven, and peace on earth to those with whom God is pleased.'"*

And 1 Timothy 2:3-4: *"This is good and pleases God our Savior, who wants everyone to be saved and to understand the truth."*

I prayed about this burden for days, and it was confirmed to me three times thereafter from three different sources. Only then did I share the burden with my husband and our friends, our former home group leaders, and I shared it with our current home group leaders too. It was received by my husband and our friends with affirmation and unity. In fact, our home group leader liked the idea so much that he said he would like to give his testimony as well. That was a real joy for me and the fourth confirmation!

The day arrived sunny and bright, and I was more nervous than I was on my wedding day. It is probably the scariest thing I have ever done, but I believe God had told me to do this, so I put my fears in Him and trusted Him to do the work. "'Not by might, nor by power, but by My Spirit,' says the Lord of hosts" (Zechariah 4:6 NKJV). It was a great day and we had a good turnout, but I could never have done that without the support and encouragement and more importantly, prayers of my Christian friends. They were wonderful and paved the way for me to do the talking, which is what I did, followed by Kevin, my late nephew Devon, his friend Leigh, and Allen (not his real name), our home group leader.

Our testimonies were followed by a feast and a time of fellowship. No one came forward to give their lives to the Lord, but God assured me that I was not to focus on what didn't happen, but rather on what did happen in the spiritual realm. I could have been disappointed and questioned whether I had heard God correctly, but there and then I decided to believe God and not the accusations of satan's voice telling me that I had not heard from God and now I had made a big fool of myself.

To this day I still believe that all my family and extended family will be with me in Heaven one day because of the promise in Isaiah 55:8-11 given to me by God that day:

"My thoughts are nothing like your thoughts," says the Lord. "And my ways are far beyond anything you could imagine. For just as the heavens are higher than the earth, so my ways are higher than your ways and my thoughts higher than your thoughts. The rain and snow come down from the heavens and stay on the ground to water the earth. They cause the grain to grow, producing seed for the farmer and bread for the hungry. It is the same with my word. I send it out, and it always produces fruit. It will accomplish all I want it to, and it will prosper everywhere I send it."

And James 5:16: *"The earnest prayer of a righteous person has great power and produces wonderful results."*

These were the verses God gave me after this significant occasion.

That was in November, and in January I emailed B and asked her to pray for me, as I felt led to start a women's Bible study group. She encouraged me and said that was a great idea. In February, I started my first women's Bible study group. I'll never forget how humbled I felt that God had chosen me to lead a Bible study group. I have no formal biblical qualifications, just my own dedicated time I spent studying the Bible. I loved God even more for His trust in me.

Even though I never had any formal qualifications or even educational qualifications, I was always a diligent student. I loved learning my heart's desire, which was the Bible. Researching and studying the Word of God was the highlight of my days at that time. The more I researched and discovered the truth of God's vast and indescribable love for His children, the more I loved God and wanted to go out and share that love with others. I felt exhilarated, alive, and full of joy.

Several women of varying ages from different churches and from all walks of life attended that first introductory meeting. After six months, a core group of seven women gathered together twice a month at my house to study the Word of God. Our first study was from the book *Her Name is Woman: Book One, 24 Women of the Bible* by Gien Karssen. For me, it was the beginning of ministry as I knew it and I was elated. I felt as though I was exactly where God wanted me to be, and the fit felt good.

A NEW CHAPTER

In October 2006, I began a chapter in my life that I had always dreaded—menopause! I had peri-menopausal symptoms and began to experience feelings of depression and oppression. One night after our Bible study meeting, I was taking a bath when suddenly a wave of dark depression came over me, and at the same time, these words came into my mind: *Who do you think you are to teach Bible study? You are not fit to be alive. You should take your life. No one will miss you, because you're worthless.*

I was hysterical as I called out to my husband for help. He could hardly make out what I was saying, I was crying so much. He saw how hysterical I was and sat me down. With his arms tightly around me, he began to pray. He prayed with an authority that came straight from the Holy Spirit. As he prayed, I felt a distinct lift of the oppression and darkness and I slowly began to feel a peace and lightness come over me. By the grace of God, I eventually calmed down. The darkness left me, and I slept soundly that night.

The next morning, I phoned one of the women from my group, who was also a pastor. I asked her if we could meet to discuss what had happened the previous evening. We met the next week and I told her what had happened to me after Bible study. I also told her that I felt sure I was starting menopause and that at some stage when I was quite a lot younger, I had made a promise to myself that if the day ever came when I would need Hormone Replacement Therapy (HRT), I would not take it as I didn't think it was safe. I was sure God could take it away if I just prayed about it.

She said she was glad I had called her and told me that she had also said the same thing at that stage in her life. Then she laughed and said, "Leonie, you cannot just pray away nature. God made women a certain way, and we have to go through menopause, not around it!" She suggested that I seriously reconsider my decision not to take HRT. On her advice, I made an appointment with a menopause specialist, and he explained the pros and cons of taking HRT. He advised that, provided HRT was managed on a regular basis, I would be fine. And so began my journey of hot flashes, weight gain, and mood swings. [Sigh!] Thankfully, I never again suffered the dark depression that I suffered that night. Thank You, Lord, for wonderful friends who give good wisdom and counsel from You.

"But God" Chapter 13

I've said it before, but it's worth repeating—we have an enemy that will do anything he can to derail us from God's purpose for our lives. This wasn't the first time he had come against me and it probably would not be the last. "But God" bought our victory with the sacrifice of His Son Jesus on the Cross. Satan has no hold over us and no legal right to attack us if we are living in Christ, which I was. Not that that fact stops him from trying. He has been defeated and He has no power over our lives. I realize it could have been so different if my husband had not used wisdom and taken authority over the evil that tried to pervade my life that night.

A word of caution here: know the Word of God. Ephesians 6:10-18 tells us that we do not fight against flesh and blood, but principalities, powers and the rulers of the darkness of this age, against spiritual hosts of wickedness in the heavenly places. Spiritual wars must be fought with spiritual weapons, and the Word of God is your most powerful spiritual weapon. It is alive, active, and sharper than any two-edged sword (Hebrews 4:12). The Word of God goes out in power and will accomplish what it's been sent to do—it will not return void (Isaiah 55:11).

The night that I've just shared with you followed an afternoon of healing and deliverance of one of the women in the group who had succumbed to sexual immorality and was suffering because of it. What I'm saying is that there had been a breakthrough in the spiritual realm; and it's been my experience that a spiritual battle follows a spiritual breakthrough. Be prepared, not paralyzed!

Verses to Meditate on and Memorize from Chapter 13:

➤ Ephesians 6:10-18 The Whole Armor of God: *A final word: Be strong in the Lord and in his mighty power. Put on all of God's armor so that you will be able to stand firm against all strategies of the devil. For we are not fighting against flesh-and-blood enemies, but against evil rulers and authorities of the unseen world, against mighty powers in this dark world, and against evil spirits in the heavenly places. Therefore, put on every piece of God's armor so you will be able to resist the enemy in the time of evil. Then after the battle you will still be standing firm. Stand your ground, putting on the belt of truth and the body armor of God's righteousness. For shoes, put on the peace that comes from the Good News so that you will be fully prepared. In addition to all of these, hold up the shield of faith to stop the fiery arrows of the devil. Put on salvation as your helmet, and take the sword of the Spirit, which is the word of God. Pray in the Spirit at all times and on every occasion. Stay alert and be persistent in your prayers for all believers everywhere.*

Journal your thoughts:

_____

_____

_____

_____

_____

_____

_____

_____

_____

_____

Journal your prayer:

_____

_____

_____

_____

_____

_____

_____

_____

_____

_____

Chapter 14

A New Season

Life is trying things to see if they work. –Ray Bradbury

Kevin and I decided to relocate to the Western Cape in 2008. As I was working on contract at the time, Kevin left before me. On December 1, 2008, a friend of mine, Sharon (not her real name) and I left Johannesburg at 5 a.m. and headed for Plettenberg Bay. The plan was for Sharon to travel with me and then enjoy a vacation with us for two weeks. She also took the opportunity to attend a week's conference at Mount Carmel in Victoria Bay, a stunning area on the Garden Route. Our journey was relaxing and fun and we shared so much of our walk with the Lord during our trip. We stayed overnight at a cheap and cheerful bed and breakfast inn on the way; after a delicious dinner and more sharing, we turned in and had a restful night's sleep.

We arrived two days later in sunny Plettenberg Bay and to a big emotional welcome from Kevin. I was beginning to feel a sense of peace and joy come over me and started to think that maybe moving to Plettenberg Bay wasn't such a bad idea after all. I began to visualize with excitement and anticipation what God was going to do in and through us in this new season of our lives.

Kevin had chosen a lovely three-bedroom duplex with a view of the sea from our room upstairs. And the best part was that the church was literally across the road from our house. The next day we all went to this new church my husband had found, and we were welcomed enthusiastically by several people, which felt good. It turned out that Kevin had made a good choice after all, as that church was to become our new spiritual home for the next two years.

We wasted no time at all in joining a home-group, and before long we were part of the community and well entrenched in our fellowship group that met every week. As I wasn't working, I wanted to get involved in a women's group; and to that end, I contacted the church and was put in touch with a woman who was to become one of my treasured mentors. Amy (not her real name) was the Director of Fellowship Groups, Counseling, and the Teaching Ministry. I learned a lot from her while we were in Plettenberg Bay. Amy and Grace (not her real name) had been leading a women's group through a ministry called Women's Auxiliary at the church for many years. These two beautiful women of God would also become my spiritual "moms" while I was in Plettenberg Bay. At the time I joined the women's group, Amy was in the process of changing group dynamics and was delighted that I wanted to be part of the new vision.

After discussion, prayer, and direction from God, we eventually created two new groups: one under my leadership and the other under the leadership of another lovely woman in the group who also became a good friend and mentor.

FAMILY AND MARKET CONCERNS

We had been in Plettenberg Bay for one month when my mom phoned to say that the cancer had returned and she was going to have to undergo more, stronger chemotherapy for another six months, possibly more. I was devastated for her, especially as I wasn't going to be there to help her this time and neither were any of my brothers or sisters. Her situation weighed heavily on my heart and mind, and I had to be satisfied with phone calls and emails, which seemed so inadequate at the time. I was also missing my children and grandchildren. The months passed uneventfully, and I went back to Johannesburg for my first visit in May of that year and managed to spend some quality time with my family.

As the months progressed, I was asked to also take over the leadership of a group of elderly, frail, but precious people at an old-age home once a week, which was not only a pleasure for me, but a huge privilege too.

To watch how those folk, some of them well into their 90s, were still keen and excited to know more of the things of God often brought tears to my eyes and to my knees in prayer for them all. These groups gave me so much pleasure, and I looked forward to our time together each week.

However, our happiness was marred by the fact that the property market was totally depressed, particularly with vacation homes, which made up 60 percent of the market in Plettenberg Bay. This caused great conflict in our marriage. As a result, Kevin and the other agents struggled to find buyers for the vast amount of stock on the market, which most agencies held. We found ourselves getting deeper and deeper into debt. I felt torn between going back to work and staying at home. My conflict was the same as it had always been—I loved being in ministry and I loved the freedom to do the "Lord's work" from home.

On the other hand, I felt guilty about being a full-time homemaker when I could be out working and bringing in some money. But having said that, there wasn't much work available in Plettenberg Bay even if I did want to go back to work. The tension between us mounted each day, and I was in prayer daily to the Lord for His wisdom and guidance. I also had the help of my prayer partners, who carried the burden to the Lord daily on our behalf.

The Lord answered my prayer when the senior minister at our church phoned me to ask if I would assist him with organizing their annual conference, which was being hosted by the Plettenberg Bay church that year. His assistant was taking some leave and he desperately needed someone to help him put everything together. The job would be for three weeks, mornings only, but I felt it was an answer to prayer, and I accepted with thanks.

From the moment I took on the task, I loved it! I had never worked in a church before, except to do volunteer work, but I discovered that it seemed to be a place where, given the opportunity, I could really thrive. Other than organizing the conference, which did take up a lot of time and organizational skills, I oversaw bereavement, weddings, sermon outlines, counseling, children's church work, prayer and teaching ministry. I also assisted with the spiritual gifts, personal boundaries, and foundations courses. It was all so exciting and I enjoyed every minute.

The conference was a huge success and a blessing to all who participated. All too soon the three weeks came to an end and I handed back the reins to the secretary.

But before I left, the secretary told me that she was pregnant; and much to my delight, asked me if I would like to take over her job for four months when she went on maternity leave. I accepted with thanks and the dates were confirmed for middle of October. This was in June, so I still had four months to fill. During the time I worked at the church, I continued to teach the various groups I was involved with and I picked those up again when I had finished working. Once I was back at home, even though I had only worked for three weeks, it took a long time to settle back into my routine. I was restless not knowing whether I should look for a job or continue 'working for the Lord in ministry.' I asked the Lord for a new vision and direction regarding my work/ministry situation. Our financial situation was dire and after six months there were still no sales. I decided to put my resume out in the hopes that I would find a temporary job until October, but work was scarce in Plettenberg Bay even for a personal assistant.

THE LIGHT OF HIS LOVE

Due to the lack of income, tension between Kevin and me began to have a detrimental effect on our relationship. Most mornings I would have my quiet time at 5 a.m. on the beach. I would walk, pray, praise, and even cry some days. I would pour out my heart to the Lord, and I remember one particular day the weather was overcast and dark, so I sat in my car instead of taking my usual walk on the beach. As I sat in the car, I saw a bird walking on the sand in front of me. The bird was black and seemed out of place on that beautiful white sand. As I sat and watched the sun rise over the sea, and as it became lighter, I saw that the bird wasn't completely black, as I had first thought. It was actually a seagull but I couldn't see the white part as it was hidden from my view.

God showed me through that small observation that we are sometimes like that bird. We show our dark side—and only when we allow the light of His love and Word to shine through us, do we reveal our true selves to the world. We, as Christians, are the light in this dark world. I was definitely showing my dark side during that lean time in Plettenberg Bay, and I was intent on laying the blame squarely at Kevin's feet.

God heard complaint after complaint, day after day, as I carved a path out on the beach from continually walking the same route on a daily basis. But I have to say that I had access to friends any time of the day or night. God had really blessed me with amazing spiritual moms and sisters. There was a particular elderly lady, let's call her Joyce, who "adopted" me as her spiritual daughter. She called me her "DIL" (Daughter in the Lord) and I called her my "MIL" (Mother in the Lord). Her own daughter was married with children and they all lived in the UK. She only saw her daughter once a year when she would visit her mother in Plettenberg Bay for two weeks at a time.

Joyce opened her heart and home to me, and we spent many happy hours caring and sharing one another's lives. Most Saturdays, my MIL and I would have lunch together. I look back on those special times with love and nostalgia knowing that, as wonderful as those times were, they will never be repeated. My MIL was close to 80 years of age at that time, and she hadn't had an easy life with her husband. He was not a believer and would persecute her for her faith, even though it was done subtly. He was a good provider, and Joyce never lacked for anything. But she shared with me one day that she would happily give it all up if her husband would bow his knee to Jesus, which up until then he still hadn't done.

During my short stay in Plettenberg Bay, Joyce shared with me many insights from her younger days. She came alongside me, recognizing a little of "her younger self" in me. She was a gracious and very beautiful woman of God. Her favorite verse was Proverbs 3:5-6 from the Classic Edition of the Amplified version of the Bible:

> *Lean on, trust in, and be confident in the Lord with all your heart and mind and do not rely on your own insight or understanding. In all your ways know, recognize, and acknowledge Him, and He will direct and make straight and plain your paths.*

Family meant the world to my MIL; and even though her married life was difficult, she was always gracious and loving toward her husband, taking to heart what God says in 1 Peter 3:1-2:

> *In the same way, you wives must accept the authority of your husbands. Then, even if some refuse to obey the Good News, your godly lives will speak to them without any words. They will be won over by observing your pure and reverent lives.*

I treasure the memories I have of my relationship with MIL, and I know that no matter how many women come into my life, I'll never have another MIL quite like Joyce, that beautiful woman of God!

"But God" Chapter 14

I experienced such highs and lows in Plettenberg Bay. I often say the months I spent there were some of the best and worst times of my life. As I've spent time writing this chapter and reminiscing of the good times there, I do so with fond memories. My MIL gave me a gift for my birthday the first year I was there, and wrote these words on a heart-shaped card filled with butterflies and flowers: "Dear Lord, Thank You for weaving Leonie into the fabric of my life. Her Colorful Personality, Depth and Compassion add Richness and Texture to who I am. Please bless her. Love, Joyce"

I have this beautiful, precious card securely taped to the front of my New Living Translation Bible, and my eyes still well up with tears when I read it. She knew me for such a short time, but filled me to overflowing with love, understanding, and a wealth of wisdom. I shall never forget her.

I missed my mom terribly, especially because of what she was going through, "But God" knew that I would need a stand-in mom, and Joyce filled that role and then some. When I couldn't be with my mom, my MIL was there to give me a hug and kind words.

Perhaps there's someone to whom you need to send a card, an email, letter, or a phone call just to say, "Thank you for being there for me."

A Verse and a Song Especially for My MIL

> Philippians 4:4-8 Final Exhortations: *Always be full of joy in the Lord. I say it again—rejoice! Let everyone see that you are considerate in all you do. Remember, the Lord is coming soon. Don't worry about anything; instead, pray about everything. Tell God what you need, and thank him for all he has done. Then you will experience God's peace, which exceeds anything we can understand. His peace will guard your hearts and minds as you live in Christ Jesus.*
>
> *And now, dear brothers and sisters, one final thing. Fix your thoughts on what is true, and honorable, and right, and pure, and*

lovely, and admirable. Think about things that are excellent and worthy of praise.

And her favorite song—*Trust and Obey* (Words: John H. Sammis, 1846-1919; Music: Daniel B. Towner, 1850-1919)

1. When we walk with the Lord
   in the light of his word,
   what a glory he sheds on our way!
   While we do his good will,
   he abides with us still,
   and with all who will trust and obey.

Refrain:

Trust and obey, for there's no other way
to be happy in Jesus, but to trust and obey.

2. Not a burden we bear,
   not a sorrow we share,
   but our toil he doth richly repay;
   not a grief or a loss,
   not a frown or a cross,
   but is blest if we trust and obey.
   (Refrain)

3. But we never can prove
   the delights of his love
   until all on the altar we lay;
   for the favor he shows,
   for the joy he bestows,
   are for them who will trust and obey.
   (Refrain)

4. Then in fellowship sweet
   we will sit at his feet,
   or we'll walk by his side in the way;
   what he says we will do,
   where he sends we will go;
   never fear, only trust and obey.
   (Refrain)

Journal your thoughts:

_____
_____
_____
_____
_____
_____
_____
_____
_____
_____
_____
_____
_____
_____
_____

Journal your prayer:

_____
_____
_____
_____
_____
_____
_____
_____
_____
_____
_____
_____
_____

Chapter 15

I Earned an "MBA" in Marriage

A bad attitude is like a flat tire. You can't get very far until you change it. –Unknown

At this stage I must say that our marriage was on *the rocks*. I was ready to run away—again. Instead, I decided to get some counseling. After each session, I journaled what was said and what I felt God had shown me. At the same time, my counselor recommended that I do the 12 Steps to Recovery Program. This program is based on the principles used in the Alcoholics Anonymous (AA) groups, but has been adapted for use in the Christian church. I took her advice, enrolled in the program, and for the next thirteen weeks journeyed to recovery and to discovering who I was.

To say that I was astounded at what the program revealed week after week was an understatement! I never realized that I was a woman who "loved too much." That I was a "rescuer," a "co-dependent" and a "control freak." My counselor was kind to me as she put it another way. She said that I should not feel despondent about what I was discovering about myself, because even though I was doing the wrong things, a lot of the time, I was doing them for the right reasons; there was hope. In addition, she said that I was too hard on myself. Both people in a marriage are imperfect people. Often and a lot of times unintentionally, they hurt each other by saying and doing things that are hard to forgive.

Since I've been saved, I have come across many couples who wish they had never married in the first place. Conflict is going to happen. It's inevitable. But with God's help, conflict can be resolved. My counselor showed me how to deal with conflict in my marriage through the 12 Steps. I must be honest and say that the 12 Steps, although very relevant, struck a nerve. Things that I hadn't thought of for years, and I thought I had put to bed a long time ago, surfaced, forcing me to deal with them.

I have been counseled on numerous occasions since my salvation, and I have always had a teachable spirit. This time around, however, I found it difficult to talk about the issues from the past and to face my insecurities and inadequacies in the 12 Steps Program. I started resenting the group discussions and I didn't feel comfortable sharing about my past like I had done at other similar groups. I even thought of opting out of the program altogether.

Thankfully, I didn't.

Throughout the time I was in the program, Kevin and I were hardly communicating. I was too wrapped up with my own issues to do anything about our marital problems. Not that I didn't care about what was happening in my marriage; I did. At that time, though, I was more worried about the issues that were surfacing from the 12 Steps than the issues in my marriage.

DISAPPOINTMENTS

During a group session one night, we were talking about disappointments. Big subject for me. Big subject for women in general. Each group member was given a turn to talk about one disappointment in life that had turned into resentment. That was a hard task for me as I had more than one. I decided to share about the dream I had from a young age of one day getting married and becoming a full-time homemaker. When I finished sharing, one of the ladies in the group turned to me and said, "So, it didn't work out. Big deal. Get another dream. I got four before I was happy!" Not what I wanted to hear. I left there that night an angry person and not too happy about how that group discussion had played out.

Years later I reflected on that discussion and had to laugh at my bad attitude. In fact, one day while I was reading my journal notes, I realized I had a bad attitude about my marriage too. This is what came to mind:

You have an MBA in marriage, Leonie—a Major Bad Attitude! Not that I wanted to admit that at the time. It just popped into my head and I knew it was true. Let me explain why I say I had an MBA.

In my mind, I was convinced that if Kevin would only change and do what I wanted him to do, then everything would be fine. Talk about putting pressure on someone to meet your expectations and needs. No wonder the poor guy didn't know which way to turn. The more I pressured him, the more he dug in his heels—and the more he dug in his heels, the more "qualified" I became in my MBA.

During the 12 Steps Program, I traveled to Johannesburg to visit the family and to help my daughter move into her new home. It was a bittersweet time. I loved seeing my children and family, but I was torn between the issues I was facing in Plettenberg Bay, as well as the concerns with my mom's health and the problems with my marriage. During those days, all I could do was rely on the Holy Spirit's help, as it says in Romans 8:26-27 (NKJV), as I did not know how or what to pray.

> *Likewise the Spirit also helps in our weaknesses. For we do not know what we should pray for as we ought, but the Spirit Himself makes intercession for us with groaning's which cannot be uttered. Now He who searches the hearts knows what the mind of the Spirit is, because He makes intercession for the saints according to the will of God.*

Eventually October arrived and I began my temporary assignment at the church. I was kept busy with all the courses, Bible study groups, and my daily work. Thankfully, that left little time to dwell on my MBA. When I started working at the church, my husband had a breakthrough in sales. He sold three houses in one month. Although it would take another three months before he would receive his commission, there was much celebration at his workplace. The commission from the sale of the three properties helped to lift the tension in our home, but we both knew the real issues were brewing beneath the surface, as the root had not been dealt with.

The 12 Steps Program required a few hours a week of homework time. We were encouraged to complete assignments each week, which was basically putting down on paper our past issues in order to bring them out in the open for discussion and hopefully resolution. If we could not deal with issues in the group discussions, we were encouraged to see a counselor. Throughout the program the need to deal with the root was emphasized. The reason being, that unless the root was dealt with, healing could not take place, and therefore no fruit.

This was, however, much easier said than done. I found that as soon as I sat down to work through my homework, all I could see was a huge mountain. After writing down one or two sentences, I would give up and make excuses not to finish the assignment. That pattern continued throughout the 12 Steps; consequently, it took a long time to complete the assignments. More about the assignments later.

BURNOUT

After a month of working at the church, it occurred to me that due to everything that had happened with my family, our relocation to Plettenberg Bay, the constant strain of financial burdens, marital issues, and even leading various groups had taken its toll on my health. I was constantly tired and realized that I had severe burnout. My counselor suggested I hand over some of my responsibilities and step down from leadership for a time, which left me with the work at the church.

At the end of December 2009, at the same time I was due to finish my temporary assignment, a job for a personal assistant was advertised in the local paper. I put my resume in straight away and was contacted for an interview shortly after. Following a second interview, much to my delight, I was given the job. As Kevin was expecting his commission to be paid in the beginning of January and I was due to start my new job the middle of January, we decided to go to Johannesburg for a week to spend some time with our children and family.

We had a lovely time with family and friends. People noticed, however, that I had one foot in Johannesburg and one foot in Plettenberg Bay. I was looking forward with excitement to my new job, but I was not looking forward to the work that needed to be done on my marriage.

It was a fact that Kevin and I had gone through some major difficulties and setbacks, and there were extenuating circumstances at play. Still, I could not see how we were going to mend all the broken places in our marriage.

In Matthew 19:8, Jesus teaches about marriage and divorce. The religious leaders questioned Jesus about why Moses said a man could merely write an official letter of divorce and send his wife away. Jesus replied that Moses permitted divorce as a concession to hard hearts, but that was not what God had originally intended.

My experience has shown me that in most divorces there is usually one person with a hard heart. Sometimes I would look at Kevin and think, *You're the one with the hard heart.* On the other hand, I'm sure he would look at me at times and say the same thing of me.

Nevertheless, when we returned to Plettenberg Bay and I began working, I just could not continue living the way we were: as though everything was fine when in fact it wasn't. I discussed my concerns with Christian friends and asked them for wisdom and guidance of what I should do. I did not want to get divorced. I also did not want to live the way we were.

Before Kevin and I got married, we both agreed that the "D" word would never be given place in our home, regardless of what might happen. At the same time, I didn't know what to do or how to move forward. I had prayed so much, but I felt that I couldn't even hear God's voice anymore. My friends gave me good godly counsel. I was grateful for their honesty and support during that time, but at the end of the day I was the only one who could make the final decision.

I once read this question: "If God were to ask you what you desire most for your marriage, what would you say?" The second question was: "In what ways do you need to change to help bring about those improvements?" I had to think about that and acknowledge before the Lord that it was not only my spouse who needed to make changes. How about you? Do you need to think about that as well?

"But God" Chapter 15

I've mentioned before that I have read many Christian books and articles about transformed lives and marriages. Each one has brought me closer to the truth of what God can do when two people are committed and submitted to Him. As couples become one in the marriage union, it is extremely difficult, if not impossible, for two people to have the same goal, yet walk in different directions. That is what Kevin and I were doing and had been doing since the day we were married.

The horrible part about all of it was that we both did not want it to be that way. We would work through a hurdle, repent before the Lord, forgive one another, and get back on track. But all too soon, the next hurdle was upon us and so the wheel went around. It was a vicious cycle—one that never seemed to end.

Having said all this however, I must add that up until that time, I had focused on all the times Kevin and I did the wrong things. There were times, however, when we listened to advice and counsel, when we listened to the Word of God and the Holy Spirit's prompting to soften our hearts and walk humbly with God and one another. When we were obedient, our home was a haven of peace and unity.

If I could have one prayer answered for marriages, it would be that every church in the world would implement marriage mentor groups for couples. Mentors, the likes of Dennis and Barbara Rainey of Family Life; Dr. James and Shirley Dobson of Focus on the Family; and Larry and Kathy Miller, to mention a few. The Bible instructs older men and women to mentor younger couples. I believe that we as the Body of Christ fail dismally in that area of ministry. All married couples need mentoring. My heart's cry and desire for Christians worldwide is that God would mobilize marriage mentor groups in the church to help couples with their marriage issues.

"But God" knew everything that we would go through and His grace covered it all. When I couldn't take anymore, I would read 1 Corinthians 10:13:

The temptations in your life are no different from what others experience. And God is faithful. He will not allow the temptation to be more than you can stand. When you are tempted, he will show you a way out so that you can endure.

I would like to share a testimony taken from the *Couples Devotional Bible* that I believe is relevant for this chapter:

Making Time
(taken from Couples Devotional Bible
NIV by Ron Hutchcraft)
Verse for the Day: Proverbs 30:21,23
Passage for the Day: Proverbs 30:1-33

Spending time with God is the time to listen to the most important voice in Heaven. Likewise freeing up time with my wife is a time to listen to the most important voice on earth. My marriage commitment implies putting Karen first, and that's almost impossible to do if she cannot get on my agenda regularly.

If Karen feels unheard, she will eventually feel unloved. And that is a dangerous state. The Bible warns "Under three things the earth trembles, under four it cannot bear up: ...an unloved woman who is married" (Proverbs 30:21,23).

Karen will not *feel* loved if I don't spend time with her. She craves a oneness that can only be built through daily debriefings. But as the delays go from days to weeks, the postponed agendas pile up and the volcano starts to rumble. Finally, a conversation starts out slowly, then it picks up momentum, knocking loose a score of larger thoughts. Every item she shares with me reminds her of another. Before long, I'm buried in an avalanche! I ask her, "Why did you wait so long to tell me all this?"

She doesn't need to answer. She tried, but I was traveling too fast to hear, or I didn't leave any time in which she could even try.

- *Are you a person who lets things pile up until there's an avalanche of emotions? What about your spouse?*
- *What time of day would be best for a "daily debriefing" between you and your mate?*

Additional Scripture Readings: Genesis 2:20-24; Ephesians 4:25-32.

This is the verse that I used for the speech I made at my youngest daughter's wedding. This is what happens when a woman feels unloved!

Verses to Meditate on and Memorize from Chapter 15:

➤ Amos 3:3 (NKJV): *Can two walk together, unless they are agreed?*

➤ Micah 6:7-8: *Should we offer him [God] thousands of rams and ten thousand rivers of olive oil? Should we sacrifice our firstborn children to pay for our sins? No, O people, the Lord has told you what is good, and this is what he requires of you: to do what is right, to love mercy, and to walk humbly with your God.*

Journal your thoughts:

_____
_____
_____
_____
_____

Journal your prayer:

_____
_____
_____
_____
_____

Chapter 16

The Separation

Love's involved with spending time together, but spending time apart can lead to loving even more. –Robert Pattinson

I had been praying about what to do regarding the problems we were having in our marriage. I didn't want to do the wrong thing *again*. On the other hand, something had to be done. I was working at the time and earning a good salary, especially for a small place like Plettenberg Bay. I felt that I needed some space to sort through the issues and to go over all the knowledge and insights I had gained from the 12 Steps Program.

I knew without a doubt in my mind that I did not want to get divorced. It was not an option and it was not the answer. But it did seem to be the only way. It was late in the afternoon and I went to see a Christian friend. She is a widow and much older than I am. She is a beautiful, humble woman of God and I valued her wisdom greatly. She had not had an easy marriage herself and there was much that I could learn from her. The one thing she loved to do was pray, she spent many hours in intercessory prayer for the saints in Plettenberg Bay and in the wider Body of Christ in the world.

I phoned her and asked if she had time to pray with me, and she said of course she would be delighted. When I arrived at her house, she was busy making dinner. She has the gift of hospitality and often opened her home to Christians from overseas. At that time, she had a young man staying with her from Germany. He had taken a sabbatical for a few months. She invited me to stay, and I accepted. It gave us more time to talk. As we worked together in the kitchen, I shared my heart with her about my struggles. She never said a word, she just listened.

She let me finish pouring out my heart and then she said, "Let's pray." She sat me down and began to pray for me. Her words were like living water as they flowed over me from the top of my head to the soles of my feet. I could physically feel the burden lifting, and I just knew (without seeing anything) that something was happening in the heavenly realm.

When she finished praying, she said, "My darling child, you know exactly what God has called you to do…so just go and do it." We had a lovely dinner together, and then I went home. The next morning, I got up early to have my quiet time. I inserted a praise and worship CD and played one song repeatedly. As I felt the power of the Living Water washing over me once again, I was aware that this was how to overcome the enemy's attacks. The song is "Redeemer," one of sixteen songs on the "16 Great Praise & Worship Classics" CD. As I listened to the words, I felt led to read Isaiah 48, in particular verses 16-20. I began praising God as my Redeemer and knew that He alone would set me free. I journaled a lot that day, and I wanted to talk to Kevin about it.

QUIET TIME TO TALK

I phoned Kevin at work and asked him if we could go somewhere quiet to talk. He fetched me, and we went down to the beach early the following morning. There were only a few people around at that time. We found a place to sit on the rocks and I began to pour out my feelings to him—honestly and without reservation. I had asked God the night before to give me the right words to say so that His truth would come out and enable us to talk honestly and openly. As I talked, I felt my words were Spirit-led. There was not the usual accusing tone nor were there angry words spoken. Just plain, open communication.

At the end of the conversation I told Kevin that I needed to be on my own for a while. I said that I did not want a divorce, that I still loved him—that would never change. I asked him if he would let me take some time to deal with the stuff that had surfaced during the 12 Steps Program some weeks previously.

I would be less than honest if I said he gave me his blessing. He obviously had some things to say himself. One of them was that he did not want to go the separation route. He felt strongly that separation was not the answer. To his mind, once a couple separated, they never got back together. I understood his reluctance; I really did. And I felt his hurt and pain. Nevertheless, I believed I had heard from God and I needed to go this route. Eventually, he reluctantly agreed to give me the time I wanted and we ended the discussion by talking through the practical things that needed to be done.

The first thing we had to do was to move out of our rented home and move into separate places. Accommodation was easy to find in Plettenberg Bay, and within a short space of time we both found alternative accommodations and moved into our respective temporary homes. I must admit, it felt awkward and lonely. I was glad that I was working all day and busy with studying at night. It helped not to dwell on us. I journaled most nights and spent early mornings and weekends walking on the beach, deep in thought and prayer.

One night I decided to tackle my assignments (from the 12 Step to Recovery Program) and start the hard work of completing them, which I did. Night after night I forced myself to work through each assignment. It was not easy and I was angry a lot of the time. It made for difficult reading, but at least I was getting it all out. One night I had a particularly painful assignment to write that I ended up writing a Psalm to God about my hurt and pain. Here is what I wrote:

A Psalm by Leonie for Shattered Dreams

Oh Lord, I feel as shattered as my dream.
The depth of pain and grief, my heart cannot contain.
I long to feel joy again—of love of peace of You.
Your Holy Spirit I miss so much, yet I know You're near.
Oh, Lord, I thank You from my heart for Your loving care.
Although I cannot feel Your Presence, I know You're always there.
So, my soul sings of Your love and my heart leaps with Your joy.
And my strength rises again, because I know You care.

During the time I spent working on my assignments, I realized I had not appropriated God's grace or forgiveness to myself, because of the divorce and the resultant hurt caused to my daughters, even though it was unintentional.

Believers know that our sins are forgiven as a result of Jesus' death and resurrection and the shedding of His blood for the remission of our sins. Nonetheless, I have also had to face the fact that even though my sins were forgiven and God removed them as far as the East is from the West and that He remembers them no more, unfortunately, the consequences of our sins remain. The aftermath of divorce is one of those consequences. I realized that there was a lot of hurt and anger in me due to disappointment of unmet expectations. I had not understood that God was the only Person who could give me value, security, and true identity; that He was the one and only source of protection, provision, and peace. I never had to perform in any way because He loved me completely and had loved me long before the creation of the world.

APPLYING WHAT IS TRUE

I never fully understood that His plans for me were for my good and not for disaster, for the future I was hoping for. I never fully understood His grace; and even now, today, this very moment, I wonder if I truly understand the fullness of His grace. I read books and studied the Scriptures; but ultimately, I missed the most important part—applying to my life what I knew to be true.

I managed to complete all my assignments during that period in Plettenberg Bay. I wouldn't call it an achievement, but I was relieved that it was done. Once I completed what I had to do and discovered what I needed to know, I put all the work at the bottom of my cupboard and I've never opened it again, as it was a painful exercise that brought back painful memories. I must admit, though, that God used these assignments to help me change my cycle of dysfunctional behavior and made me realize that my thought patterns were wrong. I needed to renew my mind to enable me to break those patterns. I received inner healing from the exercises, and for that I am truly grateful that God nudged me to complete them.

In the December before we separated, we had traveled to Johannesburg, and my dad wasn't well at that time. A check-up and tests revealed that he had a few small polyps on his colon, which were removed. Thankfully, they were benign. He was due for another examination at the end of January. My mother had finished her chemo treatments and was told she needed a break from chemo for three months. Thereafter she would have another examination. I wanted to be with my parents when they had their respective examinations, but it was not going to be easy as I had not been working at the company long enough to take leave. Nevertheless, I made a note to ask my boss when the time came around if I could take time off. My parents decided they would have their examinations at the same time to make it easier for me to be with them.

However, before that time arrived, an incident happened at work that changed my circumstances in an instant. I would like to say the detail isn't important, but that would be a lie. It was important. Still, it is something I cannot talk about. What I can say, however, is that because of what happened (and I didn't break the law or do anything immoral), I was given two weeks' notice and my employment ended. To say that I was deeply devastated by the way the matter was handled would be an understatement.

Due to this turn of events, I had to give notice at the place where I was staying, which was not fair to the lessor, but without a job I couldn't pay the rent. I was grateful to God that she was very understanding and managed to secure a tenant soon after I vacated the premises. Kevin intimated that I could move in with him, but I didn't think that was a good idea, as we would have continued in our dysfunction again, and that would not have solved our issues.

What I did was contact my daughters the next day and told them what had happened. It was just before the Easter weekend, so they said I should come to Johannesburg for Easter and spend some time with the family. It was a good idea, as I could also take the opportunity to see my parents at the same time. I told Kevin what I was doing, packed a few things, booked a flight, and arrived in Johannesburg, all within 48 hours.

Kevin was not happy that I was going to Johannesburg, but he knew the reason I was dismissed and thus he knew why I needed to go away for a while. My family was happy to see me, and I could go with my parents to their respective check-ups. I was also able to spend time with my daughters and grandchildren and to catch up with family and friends.

My family and friends were aware that Kevin and I were separated and it caused some tension with certain members of my family and certain friends. However, my stance was firm, and I was not about to explain myself to anyone. God knew my heart and for me that was all that mattered. I had His grace to get through that season and I was so grateful that nothing could take that away.

QUIET TIME WITH THE LORD

One morning when I woke up I decided to go out for the day on my own. It was a good idea to spend some quiet time with the Lord. I had so many questions about what had happened in Plettenberg Bay. My thoughts were all over the place and satan had a field day with my thoughts, as he shot those darts of doubt into my mind about the decisions I had made recently. I felt like I was in the sea being tossed back and forth by waves of doubt. I knew what the Word said about being double-minded, but I was battling to focus my thoughts on the truth of God's Word.

I spent the day talking to God about it all. I prayed, read the Word, and listened. I was desperate to hear from Him. I knew I had to apply the promise to "Be still and know that I am God" and to be at peace and believe that God was in control, even though in the natural it didn't seem like it. I journaled a lot that day and the one word that kept coming up strongly throughout my writing was, TRUST.

Proverbs 3:5-6 says, "Trust in the Lord with all your heart and lean not on your own understanding; in all your ways acknowledge Him, and He shall direct your paths" (NKJV). I knew that verse and could quote it word for word. Maybe that was the problem. I needed to meditate on it and take it from my head to my heart, then hide it there so it would become part of me.

When I returned home, I felt more peaceful than when I had left in the morning and had decided that trusting God was a good thing. Later that day a friend phoned and asked me if I would house-sit for her while she was vacationing overseas for three months. I was amazed at the timing and agreed. I then phoned Kevin and told him that because of everything that had happened, I had decided to leave Plettenberg Bay permanently and remain in Johannesburg.

We talked about the practical issues, and we agreed that he would pack up my belongings and send them to Johannesburg. He would also store our furniture until we decided what to do. He said that he missed me, loved me, and did not want to remain separated for much longer, but he was not ready to return to Johannesburg. I told him nothing had changed. I still loved him and that we could talk about him moving back to Johannesburg after my three months of house-sitting was over. He agreed.

This all happened when the World Cup Soccer games were taking place, and Johannesburg was alive with festivities and excitement. I was feeling relaxed and I rejoiced in spending quality and quantity time with the Lord. I was "still" for the first time in a long while, and I put my trust in God believing that He was in control and causing all things to work together for my good.

"But God" Chapter 16

I was relaxed and at peace. Other people weren't, especially as far as my decision to separate from Kevin was concerned. It had unfortunately caused division between some friends and family members. It made me sad that the loudest judgment came from well-meaning Christian friends. They were quick to give me their opinion about what I should or shouldn't have done in my marriage, but God's grace was missing in their judgment. (All has since been forgiven and there is no bitterness or unforgiveness from my side.)

I remember attending a women's retreat one year, and to illustrate a little of what it was like to walk in someone else's shoes, we were told to take off our shoes (it was winter time) and swap with the woman next to us. We had to put on that person's shoes and then get up and walk around a bit to get a feel of what it was like to literally walk in someone else's shoes. Whoever was brave enough gave a testimony of what it felt like to walk in someone else's shoes. There were many remarks and comments.

Some women said it felt funny. Some said it was awkward—either too big or too small. Some said it was uncomfortable and some were quick to say it was downright yucky! All in all, it was a good illustration that got the point across well! Do not judge others unless you have walked a walk in their shoes!

I wanted to argue and justify my actions, "But God" helped me to remain silent instead. It hurt, but I was determined not to allow it to sour my attitude or harden my heart. I was only able to do that because throughout the whole process, I felt a protection and an understanding from the Father like never before. I knew that if I weathered the storm and pushed through the present problem, and at the same time remained steadfast in His love, that I would be stronger at the end of it. I cannot say for certain that separating from Kevin was the right thing to do, but I'm grateful that no matter what happens, nothing can separate me from God's love. That promise kept me standing firm in my conviction.

After having told you my story of separation, I would like to comment that if you are considering separation, please consider drawing up some guidelines. For example, the separation should be for a specified, agreed-upon time, for a specific reason (such as inner healing), and at the end of the specified time, get back together so that you are not tempted to allow the separation to proceed into divorce.

Another example is to agree on a method of healing, like I did when I had to work through my 12 Step assignments and other studies. I needed alone time to spend with the Lord in order to heal from daily difficulties like frustration, anger, hurt, etc. I had to remove myself from the situation to do this work. Perhaps you might just need to be alone for a weekend of seclusion in order to hear from God.

My intention in going my separate way in the first place was to work through what I had learned over the years about how to apply God's Word and promises to the mistakes I had made in the past and to work through them so I would not go through another divorce. Surely, I had learned something over all these years? Someone close to me actually said this to me, "Surely, as a Christian woman of God and Bible teacher, you can work this out." And I answered that I could, "But God" knew I needed time on my own to do it. During the separation, unlike the other times, I never once contemplated divorce. I knew Kevin and I could get through this particular season, but I also needed the time; and I thank God that He protected us both during that time.

Verses to Meditate on and Memorize from Chapter 16

> 1 John 4:7-21 Loving One Another: *Dear friends, let us continue to love one another, for love comes from God. Anyone who loves is a child of God and knows God. But anyone who does not love does not know God, for God is love.* **God showed how much he loved us by sending his one and only Son into the world so that we might have eternal life through him.** *This is real love—not that we loved God, but that he loved us and sent his Son as a sacrifice to take away our sins.*
>
> *Dear friends, since God loved us that much, we surely ought to love each other. No one has ever seen God. But if we love each other, God lives in us, and his love is brought to full expression in us. And* **God has given us his Spirit** *as proof that we live in him and he in us. Furthermore, we have seen with our own eyes and now testify that the Father sent his Son to be the Savior of the world. All who declare that Jesus is the Son of God have God living*

in them, and they live in God. We know how much God loves us, and we have put our trust in his love.

God is love, and all who live in love live in God, and God lives in them. And as we live in God, our love grows more perfect. So we will not be afraid on the day of judgment, but we can face him with confidence because we live like Jesus here in this world. Such love has no fear, because **perfect love expels all fear.** *If we are afraid, it is for fear of punishment, and this shows that we have not fully experienced his perfect love.* **We love each other because he loved us first.**

If someone says, "I love God," but hates a fellow believer, that person is a liar; for if we don't love people we can see, how can we love God, whom we cannot see? And he has given us this command: **Those who love God must also love their fellow believers.**

➤ Matthew 7:1-5 Do Not Judge Others: **Do not judge others, and you will not be judged. For you will be treated as you treat others.** *The standard you use in judging is the standard by which you will be judged. "And why worry about a speck in your friend's eye when you have a log in your own? How can you think of saying to your friend, 'Let me help you get rid of that speck in your eye,' when you can't see past the log in your own eye? Hypocrite! First get rid of the log in your own eye; then you will see well enough to deal with the speck in your friend's eye.*

Journal your thoughts:

_____

_____

_____

_____

Journal your prayer:

_____

_____

_____

_____

_____

Chapter 17

At the Right Place at the Right Time

Just remember, God is with you. He will make everything beautiful at the right place, at the right time. –Unknown

When I lost my job in Plettenberg Bay, I wondered why I had even been offered and accepted the job in the first place—it was for such a short time. But when my dad suddenly became ill and I was able to be there for both my parents, when my other siblings couldn't, I realized that I needed to just rest in the Lord and trust that He was in control instead of trying to work things out myself.

When I wasn't visiting my dad in the hospital or visiting with my mom, I visited my daughters and grandchildren as often as I could. I spent a lot of time with the Lord, journaling, praying, and studying the Word. Still, there were days when I had doubts about my decision to separate and the way things had happened for me to be back in Johannesburg. Of course, God is sovereign; and even though He didn't cause my circumstances or my dad's illness, He was always aware of them and worked in and through them. I was really glad that I was able to be there for my parents and so was the rest of the family.

Throughout this whole ordeal, Kevin and I were in daily contact with one another and he was in the process of having some counseling and pastoral care from a pastor he had met just before I left Plettenberg Bay. This pastor offered a training course that met one evening a week, which Kevin attended and from which he was gaining valuable guidance and support. I was genuinely pleased for him and encouraged him to continue with the course, which he did. He still had not decided when he wanted to return to Johannesburg, but we were missing one another terribly.

Finally, after about three weeks in the hospital, the doctor announced one day that dad was well enough to be discharged. All praise to our Lord and Savior for answered prayer for healing.

After three long months, it seemed as though things were beginning to return to normal. As always, God's timing was perfect.

"But God" Chapter 17

I once heard a sermon on God's providence using the story of Joseph. The pastor said that even the camels that were used for the caravan of the Ishmaelites coming from Gilead, to whom Joseph was eventually sold, were born at the right time. I know that's a strange point to make, but it bore thinking about in terms of God's providence. God is omniscient and omnipotent. He is all-powerful and all-knowing. We are told in James 1:17, "Whatever is good and perfect is a gift coming down to us from God our Father, who created all the lights in the heavens. He never changes or casts a shifting shadow."

God didn't cause my dad's ill health, "But God" used the opportunity for me to be there for my parents when they needed me. And He went above and beyond that too. I had a beautiful home to live in for three months. My sister chose that time to go overseas and I had the use of her car for three months. I was able to sort out their medical bills, which they would not have been able to do themselves and in doing so, it prevented any outstanding accounts having to be paid by them personally. I was able to spend quality and quantity time with my family and with the Lord; a luxury that unfortunately doesn't happen often because of, well, because of life. I was grateful for everything and thanked God that as always, He had me in the right place at the right time.

Verses to Meditate on and Memorize from Chapter 17

> ➤ Romans 8:27-28 (GNT): *And God, who sees into our hearts, knows what the thought of the Spirit is; because the Spirit pleads with God on behalf of his people and in accordance with his will. We know that in all things God works for good with those who love him, those whom he has called according to his purpose.*

> ➤ Ecclesiastes 3:9-15 (NKJV) The God-Given Task: *What profit has the worker from that in which he labors? I have seen the God-given task with which the sons of men are to be occupied. He has made everything beautiful in its time. Also He has put eternity in their hearts, except that no one can find out the work that God does from beginning to end. I know that nothing is better for them than to*

rejoice, and to do good in their lives, and also that every man should eat and drink and enjoy the good of all his labor—it is the gift of God. I know that whatever God does, it shall be forever. Nothing can be added to it, and nothing taken from it. God does it, that men should fear before Him. That which is has already been, and what is to be has already been; and God requires an account of what is past.

Journal your thoughts:

_____

_____

_____

_____

_____

_____

_____

_____

Journal your prayer:

_____

_____

_____

_____

_____

_____

_____

_____

_____

Chapter 18

Time to Reconcile

Take off your mask, break down your walls to rebuild your marital paradise. —Marie-Violene Mertilus

After my dad returned to work and things settled down to normality, and after my friends returned from overseas and moved back into their home, other friends of Kevin and mine kindly offered for me to stay with them while I looked for a job in the North of Johannesburg. I decided to accept their offer, as I realized that most of the good, well-paying jobs were in the North. And because I didn't want to travel the distance from the East Rand every day, it made sense to find a place to live closer to work. I moved in with them and began looking for a job. I had not worked in the corporate world for many years, and a lot had changed from when I left my previous job before moving to Plettenberg Bay.

There was no shortage of jobs in the North, and they were all well paid. I had a few interviews, and it seemed I was liked and it was indicated that my skills were desperately needed, but I wasn't called back for any second interviews. This continued for a couple of weeks. I applied for more jobs in those two weeks than I ever had before. I used the Internet job sites. I followed up on referrals from friends. I even applied for jobs that I had never done before, confident that I could do them anyway. Like sales, but all I heard was, "We'll let you know," and they never did.

I began to convince myself that this wasn't the route God wanted me to go. My friends and family disagreed and encouraged me to keep on trying as something would eventually come up. My daughter very politely hinted that my resume was quite outdated and could do with some updating. I took her advice and dollied it up; and lo and behold, I had an interview through a friend from her work. I went for the interview and got the job all in the space of three days.

And then began the grind of early mornings, long days, and early nights, which wasn't going to be easy. I had been out of that cycle for nearly five years. I was, however, grateful for the job and the good pay. It wasn't a permanent job. I was on contract for three months.

Three days before I started working at this new job my ex-husband, Trevor, was rushed to the hospital after a tragic chain of events occurred. My daughters, Trevor's wife, and his family were very distraught as it happened suddenly. We contacted our prayer partners and beseeched God for his healing. Three days later, however, the day I started my new job, he passed away. He left a devastated wife, three daughters, and extended family, not to mention his close friends that were as brothers to him. As I had just started working, I was not able to be there for my daughters, and it broke my heart to see their pain.

I don't want to make his untimely death about me, but it brought back so many memories and stirred up painful regrets in my heart. I wasn't a Christian when we got divorced and the situation was obviously different then, than it was at the time of his death. However, I had written to him when I became a Christian to ask for his forgiveness, and I felt at peace that we managed to reconcile our differences. When my girls told me that he wasn't going to make it, I asked them to tell him that I loved him, with the love of the Lord, and that I was sorry for the pain I'd caused him all those years ago, which they did.

On the days that I could see my daughters, we spent the time crying, reminiscing, and just talking through it all. At the funeral, my younger daughter gave the eulogy, which was so heartwarming. The one thing she said, which touched my heart, was that she had no regrets. That her relationship with her father, right up to the moment he died, was loving, sincere, and honest. The same was said for my eldest daughter. It was a tragedy and has left a huge void in the lives of my children, sons-in-law, and our grandchildren. It is comforting to know that even though we don't understand the why of the situation, God is still in control, and His ways are higher than ours.

TOGETHER AGAIN

At the same time as this tragic event happened, Kevin decided to move back to Johannesburg. We had been in discussions about his decision beforehand, and we both agreed that it was time to reunite, put our separation behind us, and move forward with God at our side.

It was good timing as he was there for me when I started my new job. It was strange being back together again. I could no longer do my own thing and come and go as I pleased, as it says in 1 Corinthians 7:34, "...But a married woman has to think about her earthly responsibilities and how to please her husband." Before Kevin moved back to Johannesburg and while I was praying about whether this was the right time for him to move back, I read a quote (I think a Chinese proverb), that goes something like: "When the student is ready the teacher will appear."

The question I asked myself after I read that quote was, *Am I ready to have Kevin back in my life? If I am, I better be ready to be a wife again in the full sense of the word, and there is no going back.* So, that day I made a commitment that marriage wasn't an agreement, it was a covenant with God—and a covenant with God was serious business.

From the time Kevin returned, we began looking for a home and found one five weeks after he arrived. It certainly wasn't the ideal place, but it was furnished, affordable, and it was a stone's throw from my new job. That became our new home until we could afford to build up our finances and find something more suitable. Our furniture was back in Plettenberg Bay, in a secure storage unit. As the cottage was only one room, we had to be creative for some privacy. I began to have my quiet times outside in the garden at 5 o'clock in the morning; and as winter approached, my spot changed to inside my car with a steaming cup of coffee!

My new job was very stressful and extremely busy. I was an administrator at a training college. Deadlines were of utmost importance, and we worked from one deadline to the next all day. At the same time, Kevin also started a new job, and we were both exhausted by the end of the day. In his new job, Kevin was working some evenings and most weekends—Friday nights, Saturdays, and Sundays.

Spiritual Home

When I was staying with our friends before Kevin returned, I began to pray that God would lead me to a church that we could make our spiritual home. One Sunday in September, I visited a church in Bryanston and immediately had a sense that it was home. I also met friends there from my previous church, whom I hadn't seen for about three years. I began to attend every week; the more I visited, the more I loved being there. When Kevin returned to Johannesburg, I told him about the church. The first Sunday he was back we went to church together and he said he felt the same way I did. So there and then we decided to make New Life Church in Bryanston our new spiritual home. Eight years later, we both still feel our decision then was the right one, and we love our church family.

Many people watched our reunion. As mentioned in the previous chapter, people were quick to judge my decision, and they were now skeptical about whether we would have a successful and more importantly, lasting reunion. There are no guarantees in life, but one thing Kevin and I knew, we loved God more than our struggles and our issues. Our covenant with God and one another was for better or for worse, and no matter how many struggles we faced, we weren't prepared to break that covenant. We held fast to the Lord, and together we continued our journey with Jesus at our side.

Kevin will be the first person to tell you that he was not marriage material before he met Christ, but salvation and unconditional love from the Savior turned that attitude on its head. Suddenly, after salvation, marriage and family were his priorities. We certainly had our issues, but one thing I must say about my husband, he is as committed to me today as he was the day he married me. He also loves the Lord with all his heart and has no intention of leaving either the Lord or me.

He once told me that his life before Christ was only about the boys and the pub; but as the years have gone by, he knows without a shadow of a doubt that he would never go back to that single life for all the money in the world. He loves being married and couldn't imagine life without the Lord or me. Does that mean we eventually got marriage right?

Well, yes and no. We still struggled with our issues, but I can honestly say that progress and improvement have been made.

We both agreed that the decision to get back together was a good and right one. Now we had to learn to live with one another again and surrender our wills and our right to be right, to the Lord.

"BUT GOD" CHAPTER 18

According to The *Illustrated Everyday Bible Companion* by George W. Knight with Rayburn W. Ray, the word "reconciliation" means the process of bringing opposing parties or people together." It was always our good intention to put our disagreements behind us and reconcile, and we managed to do that a lot of the time. But Kevin and I still had residue from our past in our will and emotions. Many times we couldn't just let things go and drop it. One of us always had to have the last say. It was at those times when I would go off into another room or for a drive (this was my usual reaction), go over it all in my mind, justify my actions and words, and disqualify his.

"But God" would always bring me back to His Word, which was the only truth and the only words we should have been dwelling on. One of the scriptures I constantly had in my mind is found in 1 Peter 3:1-4:

> *In the same way, you **wives must accept the authority of your husbands**. Then, even if some refuse to obey the Good News, your godly lives will speak to them without any words. They will be won over by observing your pure and reverent lives. Don't be concerned about the outward beauty of fancy hairstyles, expensive jewelry, or beautiful clothes. You **should clothe yourselves instead with the beauty that comes from within, the unfading beauty of a gentle and quiet spirit, which is so precious to God.***

I had taught this verse, used the verse to speak at women's functions, and prayed it, but I still managed to avoid *living* it, from my heart. The times that we were at loggerheads with one another and this passage came to mind, I would act like Lysa TerKeurst did when God spoke to her about adopting her sons from Liberia—she put her fingers in her ears and said "LaLaLaLaLa, I'm not listening!" But she did adopt two boys and is very happy that she obeyed God's nudging. Seriously though, if something is precious to God, shouldn't we be taking extra special notice of that? I wanted to. Really, I did. Every time we argued, I wanted to do what I knew was the right thing, which I did sometimes. At those times, when I acted in faith, God always backed up my faith with reconciliation between Kevin and me, and the make-up was sweet. Now I just had to learn to do it all the time!

Verses to Meditate on and Memorize from Chapter 18

> ➤ Colossians 1:20 (NKJV): *and by Him to reconcile all things to Himself, by Him, whether things on earth or things in heaven, having made peace through the blood of His cross.*

> ➤ 1 Peter 5:8-9 (GW): *Keep your mind clear and be alert. Your opponent the devil is prowling around like a roaring lion as he looks for someone to devour. Be firm in the faith and resist him, knowing that other believers throughout the world are going through the same kind of suffering.*

> ➤ 1 Peter 5:8-9: *Stay alert! Watch out for your great enemy, the devil. He prowls around like a roaring lion, looking for someone to devour. Stand firm against him, and be strong in your faith. Remember that your family of believers all over the world is going through the same kind of suffering you are.*

Journal your thoughts:

_____

_____

_____

_____

_____

_____

_____

_____

_____

_____

_____

_____

_____

Journal your prayer:

_____

_____

_____

_____

_____

_____

_____

_____

_____

_____

_____

_____

_____

Chapter 19

Stirring Up the Gifts (Part 1)

Do not neglect the spiritual gift within you, [that special endowment] *which was intentionally bestowed on you* [by the Holy Spirit]... –1 Timothy 4:14 (Amplified Bible)

The year 2011 was significant for me. At the beginning of the year I went to a Christian book store to purchase a book for Kevin's birthday present, which was coming up on January 8. When I entered the store where I normally purchased my Christian books, I found that it had changed ownership and had also changed the type of books that were normally available. I couldn't find the book I was looking for. The books they stocked, although they were Christian books, were quite different to the other Christian bookstores I'd shopped at in the past. I was disappointed. I had visions of driving 10 kilometers (6 miles) or more to another Christian bookstore.

However, as I was wandering around the store I found a book that was quite out of context for the new format of that store. The book was entitled *Follow Your Heart: And Discover God's Dream for You* by Judy Petersen, which immediately said, "Buy me!" Well, it didn't really say that, but you know what I mean. So instead of Kevin getting a birthday present, I got a present instead; and what a gift it turned out to be. Judy Petersen's passion is helping women pursue their dreams. She writes from her experience as a wife, mother, grandmother, business woman, author, and speaker. Judy and her husband, Len, live in New England, USA.

I literally consume Christian nonfiction books, and I have read hundreds of them. This book was no exception, and it changed my life. It ministered so much to me that I even tried contacting the author to tell her what an impact her book had made on me. To my disappointment

I couldn't find Judy Petersen anywhere on the Internet. I then wrote to her via the address in the book. Regrettably, it was returned three months later.

The book is about women, from all walks of life, stepping out in faith and following their dreams. Some of these women gave up incredibly lucrative jobs to follow their dreams, and there were many testimonies from a variety of different women who had done just that. They testify to how fulfilled they were for taking a step of faith to follow their dreams.

When I began reading *Follow Your Heart*, 1 Timothy 4:14 came to mind and I felt God stirring up my gifts, my long-forgotten dreams and desires once again. While I was reading the book, we were having a sermon series at our church called Reinvention, which looked at our gifts and callings. I took notes; did the homework; answered the questions; and after which time, I felt God was really stirring up my gifts and telling me I needed to go and use them for His glory and for the equipping of His church.

As a confirmation, a friend asked me if I would like to give two talks: one at a women's function to be held at the end of March that year in Johannesburg and the other talk to be held in Cape Town at the beginning of June. If that wasn't exciting enough, another friend asked me if I would be the speaker at their women's ministry breakfast to be held in November of that year.

After praying about these invitations, I sensed God's prompting to accept all three invitations.

At the end of January my contract at the training college came to an end. The company wanted to extend my contract, but I wasn't sure I wanted to continue working there. There were a number of strange things going on, and I didn't feel at peace. While I was praying about what God wanted me to do, an opportunity opened at the South African Theological Seminary (SATS) as a partnership administrator. Apart from the fact that I really wanted to work at the seminary, I also took into consideration that I could be more involved in the Apples of Gold ministry with my dear friend Bev van Rensburg. Bev is a tutor at the seminary.

Following a successful interview, I felt led to accept the job and started working there March 1.

NEW YEAR, NEW HURDLES

Also in January that year, which was turning out to be a very busy time for me, I met a woman who would become one of my dearest, closest friends and mentor. Let's call her Karen and her husband, Fred. Karen and I met through a mutual friend. We quickly became close friends—joined not at the hip, but at the heart! I thank God for her and for His timing. Karen and Fred lived close to where I worked. This gave us the opportunity to meet frequently for lunch. We also met at her house for a quick bite to eat after work. Whenever we met, we delighted in sharing one another's journeys.

When we moved to the North of Johannesburg, we also moved away from our previous church and all our friends from that area. I missed those women in my life and the close fellowship and mentorship that we shared. Karen more than filled that gap.

Kevin and I were, unfortunately (and I'm ashamed to say this), back *On Divorce Row* and struggling financially once again. He had also changed his job the same time I started working at the seminary. His probation came to an end and they didn't renew his contract. I'm conscious as I write this chapter that because of what I've shared about our financial position, that you, the reader, might assume that our problems were predominantly financial. If I were reading this book, that's what I would assume too. But I have to say that although finances were a big factor, which certainly contributed to a huge part of our marital issues, there was so much more to our struggles than just financial issues. We will talk about those struggles later.

In February, a women's leadership seminar was held at my home church. The notice for it was so appealing to me. Even though I wasn't a leader at the time, I really wanted to attend. I invited my friend Karen to accompany me, and we were so glad that we made the effort to attend. The seminar was life-changing.

The seminar was led by Nancy Beach, a senior pastor from Willow Creek Church in Chicago, Illinois, USA at the time. Nancy started her talk with the subject "Defining Moments." She asked the audience to think back to a time before they turned 15 years of age. We had to recall our first defining moment. A defining moment would be a time when something significant happened in your life, whether good or bad. Something that would characterize your life and define who you were from that time on. We then had to share that moment with another woman. My first defining moment was when I realized at five years old that I liked being cared for.

My second significant defining moment happened shortly before I turned fourteen. I realized then that I wanted to be a cherished wife and mother. I wanted to save myself for my wedding night. And I wanted to live happily ever after, nurturing my husband and family. I also realized that day at the seminar that there was a ministry leader inside of me screaming to get out (Nancy's words not mine). It was quite a revelation for me, but God affirmed that in my heart. I knew without a shadow of a doubt if I was to be true to myself, I couldn't go another day without finding out more about the call that God had placed on my life all those years ago. The revelation, however, begged the question, "What now, Lord?"

In March I gave a talk at a ladies' breakfast entitled "The Beauty and Worth of a Woman." The foundation of the talk was based on 1 Peter 3:1-6 from The Message Bible version:

> *The same goes for you wives: Be good wives to your husbands, responsive to their needs. There are husbands who, indifferent as they are to any words about God, will be captivated by your life of holy beauty. What matters is not your outer appearance—the styling of your hair, the jewelry you wear, the cut of your clothes—but your inner disposition. Cultivate inner beauty, the gentle, gracious kind that God delights in. The holy women of old were beautiful before God that way, and were good, loyal wives to their husbands. Sarah, for instance, taking care of Abraham, would address him as "my dear husband." You'll be true daughters of Sarah if you do the same, unanxious and unintimidated.*

At the end of the breakfast I was amazed at how many women confided in me about their unworthiness issues—my heart went out to them. It's a major stumbling block for many women. I have come across many women who sadly live the pressure of trying too hard to wear too many hats. I know "multitasking" was the buzz word at one time; given predominantly to women. Personally, I don't believe in multitasking, although I found that out the hard way. I believe multitasking is the worst thing a woman can do.

We heap an excessive amount of guilt on ourselves due to what we do or don't do. It's unnecessary, of course, but we do it nonetheless. I think it is mainly due to the unrealistic expectations of others. We try and do everything instead of being selective, and we fail to put boundaries in place. That in turn causes us to constantly live under false guilt and condemnation.

God says He loves us unconditionally. We are His beloved daughters. We are redeemed by the blood of His Son. We are the apple of His eye. He rejoices over us with singing, and He delights in us with joy. Our worth is found in Christ alone—no other place. We do, however, need to hear that over and over again for it to penetrate our hearts and take root. I'm passionate about who I am in Christ.

GIFTS AND CALLINGS

After the breakfast talk, I began to prepare for my next talk scheduled for June 2 in the beautiful city of Cape Town. (I also visited with my brother and sister-in-law while there.) Between the end of my talk in March and my talk in June, I came across a book called *S.H.A.P.E.* by Erik Rees. Pastor Rick Warren, the author of *The Purpose Driven Life*, coined the acronym S.H.A.P.E. which is:

S = Spiritual gifts
H = Heart
A = Ability
P = Personality
E = Experiences

As I began reading that book, it was another confirmation from God that He was encouraging me and directing me to use the gifts and calling He'd given me. S.H.A.P.E. really ministered to my heart just where I was at that time and showed me once again how faithful our God really is. Ephesians 2:10 is so clear that I wonder how we don't get it: "For we are God's masterpiece. He has created us anew in Christ Jesus, so we can do the good things he planned for us long ago." I still don't get it at times. I still at times feel inadequate and unworthy of that calling. I still couldn't understand why God would want to use someone like me for such an awesome calling. In any case, the burden wouldn't leave me, and God continued to use me, despite myself. That's the wonderful grace of God.

A few weeks later, Bev gave me the title she wanted me to talk on at the conference in Cape Town. My heart sank. *Ah no,* I thought, *I can't talk about that!* My talk was to be centered on my life as a Christian mom. But that in itself wasn't the problem. The problem was that I wasn't a Christian mom when my children were growing up, and now they were adult children. What could I possibly share with these godly moms that would benefit them in any way?

I'll be honest; it caused me some sleepless nights. In the end, I handed it over to the Lord and asked Him to lead and guide my talk. After all, the Holy Spirit is the One speaking through us—we're just the vessels He uses for His purpose. After I'd settled that in my heart, I felt a peace and even an excitement as I began preparing for my talk.

The passage that God gave me was Titus 2:3-5, "Similarly, teach the older women to live in a way that honors God. They must not slander others or be heavy drinkers. Instead, they should teach others what is good. These older women must train the younger women to love their husbands and their children, to live wisely and be pure, to work in their homes, to do good, and to be submissive to their husbands. Then they will not bring shame on the word of God."

Those verses helped me put my message across in a way that cautioned the listeners, particularly the young moms, about how absolutely fundamental it is to train their children in the way of the Lord from a young age.

We were blessed to hear three other speakers over that wonderful weekend. I listened to their talks and admired the way they had all trained their children in the way of the Lord when their children were growing up. They had incredible testimonies to share, and it was good to hear (in a good way) that even though they'd been Christian moms throughout their children's lives, they had certainly not got it right a lot of the time. They had also experienced times of heartache and desperation, not knowing what course of action to take in various situations. They had to rely totally on God's grace and mercy.

Hearing their struggles strengthened me and gave me knowledge and wisdom for future ministry to children and young moms. Once again, the Lord had me at the right place, at the right time, even though I told Him at the time He surely had the wrong person! Never doubt God's timing or His way. His way is always perfect and right for each of us individually.

"Thank You, Father, for Your confidence in me. Amen!"

"BUT GOD" CHAPTER 19

From the time I was saved I've had three desires of the heart. First, to tell others about the wonderful love and saving grace of God. Second, to bring glory to God by the way I live my life, and third, to use the spiritual gifts He entrusted to me to minister love and grace to the Body of Christ so that healing, hope, and wholeness take place: 1) Evangelize; 2) Disciple; 3) Equip.

At times I felt unworthy to even consider my desires, "But God" felt otherwise. I'm very grateful to God that He gave me opportunities to realize all three desires of my heart. Whether or not there was transformation in any given circumstance I may never know until I'm in Heaven one day. It doesn't matter. First Corinthians 3:6-9 says:

> *I planted the seed in your hearts, and Apollos watered it, but it was God who made it grow. It's not important who does the planting, or who does the watering. What's important is that God makes the seed grow. The one who plants and the one who waters work together with the same purpose. And both will be rewarded for their own hard work. For we are both God's workers. And you are God's field. You are God's building.*

The call in Matthew 28:18-20 is clear: to go and preach the Good News to all the world. I want to do that. I want to be part of bringing that Good News to this dying world. How about you?

Verses to Meditate on and Memorize from Chapter 19

> ➤ Matthew 28:18-20: *Jesus came and told his disciples, "I have been given all authority in heaven and on earth. Therefore, go and make disciples of all the nations, baptizing them in the name of the Father and the Son and the Holy Spirit. Teach these new disciples to obey all the commands I have given you. And be sure of this: I am with you always, even to the end of the age."*

> ➤ Romans 12:6-14: *In his grace, God has given us different gifts for doing certain things well. So if God has given you the ability to*

prophesy, speak out with as much faith as God has given you. If your gift is serving others, serve them well. If you are a teacher, teach well. If your gift is to encourage others, be encouraging. If it is giving, give generously. If God has given you leadership ability, take the responsibility seriously. And if you have a gift for showing kindness to others, do it gladly. Don't just pretend to love others. Really love them. Hate what is wrong. Hold tightly to what is good. Love each other with genuine affection, and take delight in honoring each other. Never be lazy, but work hard and serve the Lord enthusiastically. Rejoice in our confident hope. Be patient in trouble, and keep on praying. When God's people are in need, be ready to help them. Always be eager to practice hospitality. Bless those who persecute you. Don't curse them; pray that God will bless them.

Journal your thoughts:

Journal your prayer:

Chapter 20

Stirring Up the Gifts (Part 2)

Do not neglect the spiritual gift within you, [that special endowment] *which was intentionally bestowed on you* [by the Holy Spirit]... −1 Timothy 4:14 (Amplified Bible)

As mentioned in the previous chapter, God was allowing me to use my gifts at various places to bring salvation, healing, and wholeness to women. As I continued to seek Him for places to use my gifts, He continued to minister to me through the books *S.H.A.P.E.* and *Follow Your Heart*, which I was reading at the time. It turned out that 2011 was a year for finding and reading good books. During the month of June at the book club I belonged to, I read a book titled *Legacy Now: Why Everything about You Matters* by Phil Munsey. Munsey's book is about the impact we will have on our children and grandchildren and generations to come. I want to be a woman who sows into the next generation, including mine, and I pray that the life I live and the works I do will be a legacy for generations to come.

A few months after my talk in Cape Town, my friend Bev asked me if I would be the MC at her annual women's retreat, which was being held the last weekend in October. The ministry she leads is called Apples of Gold.[1] Betty Huizenga started the Apples of God mentoring program in 1995. It is a six-week program and originally designed for the women of her church in Holland, Michigan. *Apples of Gold* was published in March 2000 by Cook Communications Ministries. Bev brought the ministry to South Africa under the guidance of Betty Huizenga (who now resides in the USA), and the ministry is based on the biblical mentoring guidelines in Titus 2:3-5.

I had been attending Apples of Gold retreats for eight out of the ten years that it had been in existence and felt privileged to be part of this wonderful ministry. For the purposes of the retreat, Bev said we would be ministering around the same theme as the conference we had in Cape Town—"Mothers and Daughters," including, "Spiritual Mothers and Daughters" and "Surrogate Mothers and Daughters."

I've always had a heart for thirty-something women, possibly because my daughters are that age. From the time I began ministering, I noticed that the women were predominantly thirty-something, or as they're known today Generation X women. I was at a work conference recently and was amazed to read this statement: "Africa now has the fastest growing middle class in the world, with 90% of its population under [the age of] 35" (Deloitte & Touce). At the retreat, Bev asked me to lead a group of women that age, as I had some experience with "Generation Xers." Some of those women were not even Christians and that was even more exciting for me to share the love of Christ with those seeking to know more.

For the group discussions, we used Shaunti Feldhahn's DVD *Exposed* and her book *For Women Only: What You Need to Know About the Inner Lives of Men.* I have to be honest, when I heard we were using this DVD, my first thought was, *Really? Again?* I'd seen it three times already and wasn't sure that I wanted to talk through it a fourth time. I thought, *Been there—done that*, and didn't think I needed any further teaching on that subject! Wow, I really needed to humble myself and repent before God. God was about to teach me a BIG lesson on humility.

First, I should never have stepped onto the stage when I thought I knew everything, thought I'd arrived. In my experience, I have found that if we know a certain passage, verse, or Bible story really well, we tend to pass over it too quickly; and when we do that, we miss out on what God is trying to teach us through that passage—for that particular time in our lives. That's what happened to me.

Second, we need to heed the warning in Proverbs 16:18, "Pride goes before destruction, and a haughty spirit before a fall." I went before the Lord and repented of my pride. I humbled myself and began to really study Titus 2:3-5 again—and I was blown away by what God showed me.

SHEKINAH—GOD'S VISIBLE GLORY

The weekend arrived and a group of us traveled together to the lodge.[2] There were about 100 women plus young adults and children. The women came from many different regions and cultural backgrounds. There was an air of excitement and anticipation about what God was going to do. My friend Karen and I shared a room. A few days before the retreat, she'd shared with me her reservations about attending the retreat. She was questioning whether God had really called her to be there. I could relate to her reservations, because I wasn't sure that I should be there either. God, however, knew exactly what He was doing by bringing us to that conference. He was about to do a new thing in both our hearts!

Whether we were supposed to be there or not, we were in awe of God's creation at Mabula Game Lodge—Shekinah (God's Visible Glory), and we were determined to enjoy every moment. Mabula Game Lodge is a distinctly African safari destination. An extraordinary encounter with South Africa's bushveld. Mabula is a two-and-a-half-hour drive from Johannesburg in the malaria-free Waterberg region of the Limpopo Province.

After dinner on the first evening, we celebrated Apples of Gold's tenth anniversary with testimonies and prayer. Various women were also presented with Apples of Gold books, including the Apple Seeds books for children. The weekend continued with group discussions on Mother and Daughter relationship highlights, disappointments, expectations, and ideas of ways in which to minister God's love into situations.

One of the things that God did in my heart through Shaunti Feldhahn's DVD *Exposed*, was help me to realize that I had not always respected my husband—not the way God instructs wives to do. Nor had I ever told him that I was proud of him. Feldhahn's book *For Women Only* explains the question, "What's going on in a man's mind?" From the book's back cover:

> From their early days, every woman has struggled to understand why males behave the way they do. Even long-time married women who think they understand men have only

scratched the surface. Beneath a man's rugged exterior is an even more rugged, unmapped terrain. What bestselling author Shaunti Feldhahn's research reveals about the inner lives of men will open women's eyes to what the men in their life— boyfriends, brothers, husbands, and sons—are really thinking and feeling. Men want to be understood, but they're afraid to "freak out" the women they love by confessing what is happening inside their heads. This book will guide women in how to provide the loving support that modern men want and need.[3]

I was speechless when I realized that my husband needed to hear from me that I was proud of him even more than the words, "I love you." I was also relieved to know that I was not the only wife who discovered that. One by one, women went to the front of the hall weeping in repentance before the Lord for the way they had disrespected their husbands. One by one we asked the Lord to renew our hearts as we returned home to ask our husbands' forgiveness and a commitment to submit to them and honor them as unto the Lord. It was a defining moment for me and for Karen, as we realized how much we'd taken for granted the men God had blessed us with.

SHAPE

Three weeks later I was on the platform again, this time talking about S.H.A.P.E., as explained in the book of the same name. The title for my talk I found in a magazine. At that time my twin grandsons were three and a half years of age and two very busy boys indeed. My daughter and son-in-law had gone away for the weekend, and Granny and Grandpa were given the privilege of babysitting. Whenever we looked after them, Friday nights were always filled with excitement and loads of energy. By Sunday midday, however, it was a whole different ball game; by that time, we were all totally wiped out. That's how I found myself on Sunday, physically and mentally exhausted, and eagerly awaiting Mommy and Daddy's arrival to take those two energy bunnies off our hands.

While waiting, I decided to chill, and mindlessly paged through a magazine. I climbed onto the hanging basket seat, positioned in front of a huge glass door that overlooks a dam and the beautiful Magaliesberg Mountains. I started aimlessly paging through the magazine titled *SHAPE*.

It was dated 2007, about four years out of date (at that time). I wasn't planning on actually reading the magazine, so I didn't mind that it was outdated. I just wanted something to pass the time. As I flipped through the pages, I glanced through food, fitness, sports, weight loss, beauty, and overall healthy living articles. Some information I took in and others I disregarded. When I got to about the middle of the magazine, of a sudden I came across an article that caught my attention—"Women Who SHAPE Our World." Obviously, the word "Our" meant South Africa.

I looked at the title again and thought, *I would love to be featured in an article like this; as a woman who helps shape the world.* The article featured a dietician, an athlete, a journalist, an environmentalist, a surgeon, and a businesswoman. Six women who had found their way into this magazine; they had helped shape South Africa in one way or another. That article title became the title I used for my next talk— Women Who S.H.A.P.E. Their World.

We are all able to S.H.A.P.E. our world, our areas of influence, if we really want to. Anything to do with using our God-given S.H.A.P.E. is my passion, and so whenever I present this talk, I can literally feel the anointing flowing. I encourage areas of service in the local church and the wider Body of Christ.

I want to end this chapter by thanking the different churches where my husband and I have worshipped, and especially to our current Senior Pastors Chris and Lisa Stark for their hard work and dedication in teaching, pastoring and caring so faithfully for the congregation at New Life Church in Bryanston.[4] Together with the other pastors, elders, staff, and leaders at New Life Church, and for always encouraging us to use our gifts of teaching, helps, serving, etc. We love and appreciate you all very much!

"But God" Chapter 20

One day I met a Christian woman who opened a home for abused women and children. She had a passion to see women healed and restored, and that's my heart too. However, the difference is that this woman was herself an abused woman and her mission was to see women restored and integrated back into society without their husbands. My heart, on the other hand, is to see marriages restored. I say that knowing that in some cases that is just not possible, but we'll talk more about that in a later chapter.

The point I want to make here is that we all have issues regarding the hurt we've experienced from our past. Unfortunately, people do sometimes take that prejudice into ministry with them, ministering sometimes with their own agendas.

"But God" uses us despite our imperfections and discrimination. He uses us because no matter what you and I might think or do, God's purposes prevail. The bonus is that while we're about doing our ministry and calling, God is working in us too. God's grace supersedes all our biases, agendas, and hurt, and He works it all together for the good of those who love Him and are the called according to His purpose for them. Thankfully, only He knows our hearts and His eyes go to and fro the whole earth, looking for those who are willing to be sent.

Verses to Meditate on and Memorize from Chapter 20

> ➤ Philippians 2:12-14 (NKJV): *Therefore, my beloved, as you have always obeyed, not as in my presence only, but now much more in my absence, work out your own salvation with fear and trembling; for it is God who works in you both to will and to do for His good pleasure. Do all things without complaining and disputing*

> ➤ Philippians 1:12-18 Paul's Joy that Christ Is Preached: *And I want you to know, my dear brothers and sisters, that everything that has happened to me here has helped to spread the Good News. For everyone here, including the whole palace guard, knows that I am in chains because of Christ. And because of my imprisonment,*

most of the believers here have gained confidence and boldly speak God's message without fear. It's true that some are preaching out of jealousy and rivalry. But others preach about Christ with pure motives. They preach because they love me, for they know I have been appointed to defend the Good News. Those others do not have pure motives as they preach about Christ. They preach with selfish ambition, not sincerely, intending to make my chains more painful to me. But that doesn't matter. Whether their motives are false or genuine, the message about Christ is being preached either way, so I rejoice. And I will continue to rejoice.

Journal your thoughts:

_____

_____

_____

_____

_____

_____

_____

_____

_____

Journal your prayer:

_____

_____

_____

_____

_____

_____

_____

_____

_____

ENDNOTES

1. Apples of Gold: Listening, Loving, Learning, Living. "A word fitly spoken is like apples of gold in settings of silver" (Proverbs 25:11 NKJV).

2. Kamp by Shekinah; http://www.shekinahkamp.co.za; accessed October 26, 2017.

3. Shaunti Feldhahn, *For Women Only* (Sisters, OR: Multnomah, 2004)

4. New Life Family Church; www.newlifechurch.co.za; accessed October 26, 2017.

Chapter 21

The Reality of Being on Divorce Row

On Divorce Row –Leonie Leo-Brewer

In January 2012, I looked back on how gracious God had been to me the whole of 2011, even with my MBA (Major Bad Attitude). I stand in awe and amazement at the wonder of God's mighty love. I didn't deserve the trust and confidence He'd placed in me. If I were God, I wouldn't have used me to minister to others.

But I thank the Lord that I'm not.

And He did.

And I am so grateful.

I wasn't at all sure what 2012 held for Kevin and me. Despite the two of us having personally experienced God's amazing grace and provision, we were still "on divorce row." We were still in a financial crisis, and we were still at loggerheads with one another, albeit not as bad as it had been. I wanted Kevin to live Ephesians 5:25: "Husbands, love your wives, just as Christ loved the church and gave himself for her" (NKJV). But, here's the irony, he really was loving me, but I just couldn't see it. I was so busy trying to take the speck out of his eye that I couldn't see to take the LOG out of my own eye! (See Matthew 7:1-5.)

When God first laid the title *On Divorce Row* on my heart, which was in 2011, I immediately knew what He meant. I didn't have to think about it or even try and work it out. It was an immediate light-bulb moment that said far more than those three little words. In fact, it summed up my married life from day one to that point. I know there are other couples out there experiencing the heartbreak of being "on divorce row", so I want to dedicate this chapter to try and explain, in my own words and experience, what happens when a couple find themselves there.

Having been on divorce row for many years has helped me understand couples who are unhappily married. Who are hostile to one another. Who sometimes act as if they hate one another. But I know from being on divorce row myself, that is not always true but rather an emotional feeling at the time. If there is even the remotest chance that your marriage can be saved, you owe it to yourselves and your children (if any), to delay the divorce and take more time to try and work through your issues.

ON DEATH ROW

I'm not a big fan of television, although I do have my favorite shows. One of them is *Crime and Investigation* (C&I), in particular, *On the Case with Paula Zahn*. I've watched this show fairly frequently over the past few years. Sometime this year I watched an episode of a man who was wrongly accused of murder and was given the death sentence. Despite his attorney's attempts to proclaim his innocence and even this man's refusal to admit guilt, even when it might have saved his own life, he was sentenced to death—he was sent to death row.

The episode of *C&I* that I watched that evening was Paula Zahn's actual interview with the man after he had been released: 10 years, 3 months, and 8 days after his incarceration. I was riveted to the TV as Paula went over the entire ordeal from start to finish, leaving no questions unasked.

You can read Ray Krone's full testimony on the Internet.[1] But I'd like to talk about one of the comments he made on the day he was released:

> I was the one hundredth person exonerated from death row. So, there was lots of media attention when I got out. On that first day, a reporter asked me, "Ray, given your faith in God, why do you think He left you in prison all those years?"

How do you answer a deep question like that? Krone thought. "Then it shot in my head," he said, "Maybe it's about the *next* 10 years."

Krone and others now lead the Witness to Innocence organization, traveling the country soliciting support to abolish the death penalty.

As I watched and listened to this interview, God showed me the parallel between being on death row and on divorce row. In answer to one of Zahn's questions about what it was like being on death row, Krone said, "Every day I sat on death row, I thought to myself, *I'm doing someone else's time.*"

Here's what I got when I heard that comment. Every day that we spend our marriages on divorce row, we are robbing our husbands, our children, and ourselves of love and happiness. We are also robbing the Kingdom and giving territory to the enemy. Every day that we spend on divorce row, we too live someone else's life. We take on someone else's identity, not our own. That is not the way God intended life and marriage to be.

Krone continued by saying that twenty-three of the twenty-four hours that he sat in his cell, he prayed that God would take his life. He said living on death row was not living at all.

I totally get that. How many times did I ask myself, "Is this really what married life is supposed to be like?" How many times did I imprison myself with negative thoughts, thinking I would be better off single? In the words of Joyce Meyer, "Some people, when they're single, wish they were married, and when they're married, they wish they were single!" I know she was joking when she made that comment, and we don't want that either, but that's how we act; and it's purely because couples are just not meant to live on divorce row when they're married.

Two Reasons

I believe I lived on divorce row for two reasons. First, my expectations of marriage were unrealistic. They were borne out of a distorted and childish picture of what marriage should be like. I now know that marriage is first and foremost God's idea—His creation.[2] The fundamental point I want to make here is that we enter into a marriage covenant with God, therefore it cannot be broken. When my husband and I participated in the marriage course at our church in Plettenberg Bay, the facilitators of the course shared with us that contrary to what people believe and use as a reason to get divorced, such as the marriage has broken down, marriage cannot break down. Marriage cannot break down because it was created by God, and anything created by God is unbreakable. Only people break down. They stop communicating. They stop trying. They stop loving one another. Then there's an obvious desire to go their own way.

I'm not denying that the decision to separate and go their own way certainly does relieve the stress and tension in the home immediately; however, that is only a temporary relief and inevitably it also becomes the catalyst for the actual parting of ways permanently.

Jesus says in Matthew 19:8 (read in context Matthew 19:4-9), that God's original intention for marriage was never meant to be this way. God intended the man and the woman to love and to complement one another until death do them part. God always had in mind good plans for marriage, not quarreling and strife, which brings me to the second reason I believe I lived on divorce row. It comes from the first part of Matthew 19:8 where Jesus pointed out that Moses permitted divorce because of hard hearts.

The second reason, I believe that in every conflict situation in marriage, there is one person with a hard heart, someone who is not willing to listen or communicate in a way that honors God and their spouse.

I'm almost sure that if I had to ask a couple in conflict which one had the hard heart, I'd get two snap answers! Now, before you throw down the book in disagreement, stay with me and hear me out. I'm not saying the instances when Kevin and I were in conflict (and there were many) were just stories that I made up. No, I'm not saying that at all. Those conflicts were real and difficult; and at that moment, the last thing I wanted to do was apply what I had learned in the marriage course, or what we'd learned at the many counseling sessions we attended over the years.

What I did want to do and what I did most of the time, I'm ashamed to say, was the total opposite, and I did it with the full force of my MBA which, as you can imagine, didn't help the situation at all!

When I look back now, especially as I've been writing this book, I've sat down many times and wept. Wept bitterly for all the wasted moments, days, months, and years. For all the heartache I had caused so many people. For every moment I lived on divorce row. For all the times I robbed my husband of my love and respect, and maligned the Word of God. Something I deeply regret. Nonetheless, while it's true that I was participating in those conflicts, that wasn't the way I wanted to act at all. I actually wanted to do the opposite. I'm reminded as I pen these words of Paul's words in Romans 7:15-25:

> *I don't really understand myself, for I want to do what is right, but I don't do it. Instead, I do what I hate. But if I know that what I am doing is wrong, this shows that I agree that the law is good. So I am not the one doing wrong; it is sin living in me that does it.*
>
> *And I know that nothing good lives in me, that is, in my sinful nature. I want to do what is right, but I can't. I want to do what is good, but I don't. I don't want to do what is wrong, but I do it anyway. But if I do what I don't want to do, I am not really the one doing wrong; it is sin living in me that does it.*
>
> *I have discovered this principle of life—that when I want to do what is right, I inevitably do what is wrong. I love God's law with all my heart. But there is another power within me that is at war with my mind. This power makes me a slave to the sin that is still within me. Oh, what a miserable person I am! Who will free me from this life that is dominated by sin and death? Thank God! The answer is in Jesus Christ our Lord. So you see how it is: In my mind I really want to obey God's law, but because of my sinful nature I am a slave to sin.*

However, once I'd repented of my sin, I was comforted that I did not need to live another day in regret and mourning; because thanks be to

God, through Jesus' death and resurrection, I have been set free from sin and death and that includes marital conflict.

I end this chapter with *The Illustrated Everyday Bible Companion's* definition of marriage by George W. Knight with Rayburn W. Ray.

> **MARRIAGE.** The union of a man and a woman in commitment to each other as husband and wife. First instituted by God in the Garden of Eden (Genesis 2:18), marriage was also confirmed by Christ (Matthew 19:5). Love for and submission to one's mate were enjoined by Paul (Ephesians 5:22-29). The love of a husband and wife for each other is symbolic of Christ's love for the Church (Ephesians 5:23-25).[3]

How is this definition of marriage similar / different to your marriage? How does it challenge you to do better / if you are on the right track, to continue to adhere?

"But God" Chapter 21

There's a saying that goes like this: "Women marry men hoping they will change, and they don't. Men marry women hoping they won't change, and they do." Sad, isn't it? But therein lies one of the biggest contributors to divorce. We shouldn't be trying to change one another—that's God's job. Our job is to work with Him to change ourselves.

There are so many great resources available today on how to:

> Have a good marriage

> Divorce-proof your marriage

> Respect and submit to your husband

> Love and cherish your wife

> Learn to be a great family (in Christ)

> And the list goes on

There are conferences, retreats, seminars, prayer meetings, and all-night vigils. There are podcasts, webcasts, webinars, Facebook, Instagram and Twitter, and yet more marriages are struggling and landing in divorce courts today than ever before in the history of humankind. Why is that? I don't know. I don't have the answers. I can only speak from my life experience and the testimonies of people I've encountered over many years.

What I have observed, however, is that women are battling to balance work and home life—which are two entirely different realms of reality. Women today must be more creative than before and more energetic. They have to learn to juggle many balls, which unfortunately leads to one of them falling. Smashing to smithereens is more like it! Sadly, it's usually the home front ball that crashes.

Today we also have the problem of men who are abdicating their roles as head of the home for several reasons. Right now, I'm acquainted with many women who would testify to this in their homes and how it has caused in some cases irreparable damage to their marriage and family.

Men should consider the consequences that abdicating their roles in the home causes.

Marriage Struggles

The following are my thoughts about why marriages are struggling, using my life experiences. First, there are definitely forces (as described in Ephesians 6:12), that are constantly working against us. But we don't need to give in to those forces. We have every spiritual weapon available to us to dispel those forces. We just need to apply them.

Second, there are external circumstances and temptations that come into play. "But God" tells us that every couple in the world has those same problems and temptations; and again, we have the tools to deal with them.

But why do some couples manage to have victory over these issues and others don't? Perhaps there is too much emphasis on the external forces when the answer is simply that we are by nature selfish and want to look out for ourselves instead of believing that we are new creations in Christ—and our attitudes and behaviors should reflect that.

"But God" loves us no matter what we've done. He doesn't condemn us or accuse us. His grace is available for all who repent and hand over our lives to Him and allow His Spirit to change us from the inside out. I want my marriage to last, and I know that if I trust God to change me by His Spirit, there is hope that my marriage will stand the test of time. I hope the same is true for you. And one day, like Ray Krone, we will be witnesses of what God can do with two hearts and a marriage committed and submitted to Him.

Verses to Meditate on and Memorize from Chapter 21

> ➤ Philippians 3:13-15 (GNT): *Of course, my friends, I really do not think that I have already won it; the one thing I do, however, is to forget what is behind me and do my best to reach what is ahead. So I run straight toward the goal in order to win the prize, which*

is God's call through Christ Jesus to the life above. All of us who are spiritually mature should have this same attitude. But if some of you have a different attitude, God will make this clear to you.

➤ 1 Corinthians 13 (GNT) Love: *I may be able to speak the languages of human beings and even of angels, but if I have no love, my speech is no more than a noisy gong or a clanging bell. I may have the gift of inspired preaching; I may have all knowledge and understand all secrets; I may have all the faith needed to move mountains—but if I have no love, I am nothing. I may give away everything I have, and even give up my body to be burned—but if I have no love, this does me no good.*

Love is patient and kind; it is not jealous or conceited or proud; love is not ill-mannered or selfish or irritable; love does not keep a record of wrongs; love is not happy with evil, but is happy with the truth. Love never gives up; and its faith, hope, and patience never fail.

Love is eternal. There are inspired messages, but they are temporary; there are gifts of speaking in strange tongues, but they will cease; there is knowledge, but it will pass. For our gifts of knowledge and of inspired messages are only partial; but when what is perfect comes, then what is partial will disappear.

When I was a child, my speech, feelings, and thinking were all those of a child; now that I am an adult, I have no more use for childish ways. What we see now is like a dim image in a mirror; then we shall see face-to-face. What I know now is only partial; then it will be complete—as complete as God's knowledge of me.

Meanwhile these three remain: faith, hope, and love; and the greatest of these is love.

Journal your thoughts:

_____

_____

_____

_____

_____

_____

_____

_____

_____

_____

_____

_____

_____

Journal your prayer:

_____

_____

_____

_____

_____

_____

_____

_____

_____

_____

ENDNOTES

1. "Ray's Story: A Death Penalty Mistake"; *The Atlantic Philanthropies*, March 19, 2012; http://www.atlanticphilanthropies.org/rays-story-death-penalty-mistake; accessed October 27, 2017.

2. Read Genesis chapters 1 and 2.

3. George W. Knight and Rayburn W. Ray, *The Illustrated Everyday Bible Companion* (Ulrichsville: Barbour, 2005)

Chapter 22

Don't Give Up—We Can Do This

... For wherever you go, I will go; and wherever you lodge, I will lodge; your people will be my people, and your God, my God.
–Ruth 1:16 (NKJV)

Can a marriage on divorce row be set free—like Ray Krone when he was found to be innocent and exonerated and set free from being on death row? Can a marriage on the rocks become a marriage on The ROCK—Jesus? The answer is yes! But there is a condition. God must be the builder of your marriage. Consider that couples in godly marriages think differently about the role of husbands and wives than those in worldly marriages.

WHAT WIVES WANT

In 2007, God laid on my heart the following talks, which I've never had the courage to present. Not because I didn't have the ability, but because He specifically told me to present the talk to men only; and I'm embarrassed to admit that despite God's promise that He would be with me, He would qualify me, and He would give me the words to say, I felt too intimidated and inadequate to minister to men. Thankfully, I'm over myself and am ready to give this talk any time God calls me to do so. The talk is entitled "What Wives Want." I have even made it easy for men to remember with this acronym: WWW.LOVE, which broken down means the following:

L is for LOVE = Love as described in Ephesians 5:25 (in context 5:23-33): *For husbands, this means love your wives, just as Christ loved the church. He gave up his life for her.* And 1 Corinthians 13:1-13:

If I could speak all the languages of earth and of angels, but didn't love others, I would only be a noisy gong or a clanging cymbal. If I had the gift of prophecy, and if I understood all of God's secret plans and possessed all knowledge, and if I had such faith that I could move mountains, but didn't love others, I would be nothing. If I gave everything I have to the poor and even sacrificed my body, I could boast about it; but if I didn't love others, I would have gained nothing.

Love is patient and kind. Love is not jealous or boastful or proud or rude. It does not demand its own way. It is not irritable, and it keeps no record of being wronged. It does not rejoice about injustice but rejoices whenever the truth wins out. Love never gives up, never loses faith, is always hopeful, and endures through every circumstance.

Prophecy and speaking in unknown languages and special knowledge will become useless. But love will last forever! Now our knowledge is partial and incomplete, and even the gift of prophecy reveals only part of the whole picture! But when the time of perfection comes, these partial things will become useless.

When I was a child, I spoke and thought and reasoned as a child. But when I grew up, I put away childish things. Now we see things imperfectly, like puzzling reflections in a mirror, but then we will see everything with perfect clarity. All that I know now is partial and incomplete, but then I will know everything completely, just as God now knows me completely.

Three things will last forever—faith, hope, and love—and the greatest of these is love.

O is for Observe. Guys need to be observant. Notice your wife's efforts at home, at work, in ministry. Her efforts with the kids, herself, her cooking skills, and so much more. Observe where she is emotionally. Does she need a kind word or act or just a hug from you? (Is it that time of the month when she's feeling tired, emotional, and fat?!)

V is for Verbalize. Once you've made your observations, be verbal about it. The more verbal you are, the better she's going to respond. We also need you to speak to us with more than those few words at the beginning and end of each day. With effort, we know you can do verbally better than what the experts say!

E is for Examine. If we were all left to examine ourselves, I don't think there would be much improvement in our characters. But if you regularly examine yourself, first before the Lord and then with a mentor, you will be better equipped to maintain WWW.LOVE.

And I encourage every man reading this book, that if you can set your goal on achieving this huge feat, and it is a huge feat, if you will make the effort to love your wife, really love her with the love of the Lord, she will not only respect you, she will respect *and* reverence you—that means notice you, regard you, honor you, prefer you, venerate, and esteem you; and defer to you, praise you, and love and admire you exceedingly! (See Ephesians 5:33 AMP). Yep, she will. Now, how can you resist that!

So now that I've mustered up the courage to put that all down in writing, I turn to wives. I'm not letting you off the hook!

Ladies, we also need to play our part in godly marriages. This is what God showed me for us wives. **RESPECT** (Ephesians 5:23-24,33): *"For the husband is the head of his wife as Christ is the head of the church. He is the Savior of his body, the church. As the church submits to Christ, so you wives should submit to your husbands in everything. Therefore, just as the church is subject to Christ, so let the wives be to their own husbands in everything. ...and the wife must respect her husband."*

R is for Respect & Recognition = Husbands need their wives to be proud of them. Genuinely proud of them. To respect the fact that they are the head of our homes and our leaders too. They've been given this awesome responsibility by God. Help them to keep to their responsibilities with a clear conscience.

E is for Encouragement & Admire. After respect, our husbands need our encouragement more than any other element in the relationship.

S is for Sex. Do I really need to emphasize this one? Men need sex, period. It's good for their health. It's good for their self-confidence. It's good for their self-esteem. It stops the temptation to indulge in pornography and adultery. Seriously friend, your husband needs sex to feel loved and desired. Don't put temptation in his path by not giving yourself to him for mutual sexual pleasure.

P is for Purposefully. Purposefully submit to your OWN husband as unto the Lord. The "S" word just mentioned usually sends women into a frenzy, but we need to get a good understanding of biblical submission (and note the emphasis on "submit to your own husband"). Once we understand submission God's way, it will revolutionize how we submit to our husbands.

E is for Enjoy. Enjoy doing things together and let him enjoy time with male friends. Psychologists and therapists recommend that married couples have shared interests; activities they enjoy doing together. But they also encourage individual hobbies too. Allow your husband to have time to relax and unwind, and while he's doing that, use that time to indulge in the things *you* love to do.

C is for Close. Be close to him when he is struggling with issues. Work, financial hardship, a besetting sin, whatever you think might be causing anxiety for him. You know the things your husband struggles with. Here's where you can be his helper, as the Bible instructs us to do. And finally,

T is for Turn. Turn him, and any frustrations you have, over to God in prayer. One of the kindest and most loving acts you can do for your husband is to pray for him. Praying with a heart of love. Prayer is powerful and life-changing, and our God is a miracle-working God—nothing is impossible for Him.

Now that we've worked that out, we need to go one step further. Don't just read these guidelines, live them. At the same time, realize that things are not going to happen and change overnight. You don't want them to anyway, as they won't last. These are actions that need to be taken one small step at a time. And in fact, you may even find as you begin to take these steps, that you're taking two steps forward, and three back. But don't be deterred. Don't get hung up on that. Just keep pushing forward in one direction, with one goal in mind. Build momentum as you go along until a point of breakthrough is achieved. And there will be a breakthrough. God is faithful. When we're being obedient to His Word, blessing will always follow.

Take Hold of Victory

I can honestly say that my transformed heart and marriage never happened in one fell swoop. There was no single defining action, no all-encompassing program, no one amazing innovation, no miracle moment. Rather, the process from being on divorce row to our marriage being on the ROCK was, I believe, due to relentlessly pushing through each and every trial with the Holy Spirit's power and the Word of God as our sword—and with much advice and counsel, much prayer and fasting, many tears, and with loving support and grace from brothers and sisters in Christ.

And you know what, a lot of the times we did all this not even with the right motives. But I take solace in the fact that God is bigger than our motives. He knows us intimately and He knows that deep down we want our marriages to honor Him. Certainly, Kevin and I did and I know you do too. We just got messed up along the way—we're human.

So, as I bring this book to an end, in this penultimate chapter, I do so with joy in my heart because despite having lived what seem like a lifetime on divorce row, we eventually took hold of the victory that Christ died for us to have and we made it to the ROCK. And if we can do it, you can too!

Don't give up. God is on your side. He's cheering you on. In the words of Hebrews 12:1 (GW):

> *Since we are surrounded by so many examples of faith, we must get rid of everything that slows us down, especially sin that distracts us. We must run the race that lies ahead of us and never give up.*

Amen!

"But God" Chapter 22

As we near the end of our journey from a "But God" point of view, I'd like to summarize what I've said up till now in key points:

- Marriage is a covenant with God and one another.

- Marriage requires time, effort, and sacrifice.

- Marriage requires 100 percent commitment and buy-in from both people.

- Marriage was God's idea—not humankind's idea. Therefore, it is important to Him, and He's our biggest supporter.

- God hates divorce.

- You have an enemy that has targeted you and your marriage for destruction. Know your enemy, but at the same time know that through Christ's death and resurrection, we already have the victory.

- There will be external factors that will come into play in your marriage, but they're not just happening to you. Learn to recognize them and deal with them God's way.

- Keep in close contact with your Christian brothers and sisters when you're struggling.

- Don't stop going to church or cell group. Don't stop praying and reading the Word.

- Share only with people who are discreet and mature in the Lord.

- Maintain a teachable spirit, especially when you're corrected or reprimanded in love.

- Don't stop believing that *nothing is impossible with God.*

- The grass is not greener on the other side. It's greener where you water it.

- Lastly, considering this, divorce is a bit like wondering if God is going to heal you from a life-threatening illness. Don't give up unless you yourself have specifically and clearly heard God tell you to do so, and then make a commitment in your heart that you will confirm it with three witnesses. God will give you the grace to be still and wait for His answer. If His answer is to not heal your body or marriage, He will give you a peace that surpasses all understanding to go through it with His grace and to surrender all in love and joy.

Verses to Meditate on and Memorize from Chapter 22

> 1 Corinthians 7:12-16 (GNT) Questions about Marriage: *To the others I say (I, myself, not the Lord): if a Christian man has a wife who is an unbeliever and she agrees to go on living with him, he must not divorce her. And if a Christian woman is married to a man who is an unbeliever and he agrees to go on living with her, she must not divorce him. For the unbelieving husband is made acceptable to God by being united to his wife, and the unbelieving wife is made acceptable to God by being united to her Christian husband. If this were not so, their children would be like pagan children; but as it is, they are acceptable to God. However, if the one who is not a believer wishes to leave the Christian partner, let it be so. In such cases the Christian partner, whether husband or wife, is free to act. God has called you to live in peace. How can you be sure, Christian wife, that you will not save your husband? Or how can you be sure, Christian husband, that you will not save your wife?*

> Romans 12:17-19 (GNT): *If someone has done you wrong, do not repay him with a wrong. Try to do what everyone considers to be good. Do everything possible on your part to live in peace with everybody. Never take revenge, my friends, but instead let God's anger do it. For the scripture says, "I will take revenge, I will pay back, says the Lord."*

> Galatians 5:22-24 (GNT): *But the Spirit produces love, joy, peace, patience, kindness, goodness, faithfulness, humility, and self-control. There is no law against such things as these. And those who belong to Christ Jesus have put to death their human nature with all its passions and desires.*

Journal your thoughts:

_____
_____
_____
_____
_____
_____
_____
_____
_____
_____
_____
_____

Journal your prayer:

_____
_____
_____
_____
_____
_____
_____
_____
_____
_____
_____
_____
_____
_____

Chapter 23

My Marriage Is on THE ROCK

Unless the Lord builds the house, they labor in vain who build it.... –Psalm 127:1 (NKJV)

Kevin and I believe that the reason we made it to the ROCK is because of our commitment to God and to our vows. Our marriage verse Psalm 127:1 was always uppermost in our minds and we did what we could to live that verse in our everyday lives.

> *If the Lord does not build the house, the work of the builders is useless; if the Lord does not protect the city, it does no good for the sentries to stand guard* (Psalm 127:1 GNT).

We've held on to that truth and pushed through the struggles, even when we didn't feel like it. I never went through with the divorce because I knew that even though on the surface things looked like they were falling apart, deep down I believed with all my heart that with God on our side, nothing was too difficult for Him to change.

Fact: God hates divorce. Fact: satan hates godly marriages and families. We know why satan hates marriages, so let's rather look at why God says He hates divorce. If we read in context Malachi 2:10-16, titled "The People's Unfaithfulness to God," we see that God hates divorce because it breaks covenant and generates violence. The people break their marriage vows.

> *Don't we all have the same father? Didn't the same God create us all? Then why do we break our promises to one another, and why do we despise the covenant that God made with our ancestors? The people of Judah have broken their promise to God and done a horrible thing in Jerusalem and all over the country. They have defiled*

the Temple which the Lord loves. Men have married women who worship foreign gods. May the Lord remove from the community of Israel those who did this, and never again let them participate in the offerings our nation brings to the Lord Almighty.

This is another thing you do. You drown the Lord's altar with tears, weeping and wailing because he no longer accepts the offerings you bring him. You ask why he no longer accepts them. It is because he knows you have broken your promise to the wife you married when you were young. She was your partner, and you have broken your promise to her, although you promised before God that you would be faithful to her. Didn't God make you one body and spirit with her? What was his purpose in this? It was that you should have children who are truly God's people. So make sure that none of you breaks his promise to his wife. "I hate divorce," says the Lord God of Israel. "I hate it when one of you does such a cruel thing to his wife. Make sure that you do not break your promise to be faithful to your wife" (Malachi 2:10-16 GNT).

Divorce destroys the family unit. The passage in Malachi says it all.

Let's recall Ray Krone's story from Chapter 21 and the question that was asked of him while he was on death row, and his answer: "Ray, given your faith in God, why do you think He left you in prison all those years?" *How do I answer a deep question like that,* he thought. *Then it shot into my head,* "Maybe it's about the next ten years."

I could relate to that statement. Often I would ask God why? Why didn't He change my situation, and the answer I received: "Trust Me and lean not unto your own understanding, in all your ways acknowledge Me and I will make your paths straight" (Proverbs 3:5-6) and "My grace is sufficient for all your needs, for My power is made perfect in weakness" (2 Corinthians 12:9).

TRUTHS LEARNED

We know God's promises are true and trustworthy—God doesn't lie. So I learned to just trust God. And what if, like Krone, it is about the next ten years, twelve years, twenty years, or whatever your number is? What if God wants to turn our messy marriage into His marriage message? Lives and marriages are transformed by the blood of the Lamb and the word of our testimony. Not that God caused our problems, but He will use them, if we allow Him and be obedient to His Word. That was the one truth I learned.

The other truth I learned was that satan has tried every trick in the book to trip me up in my marriage. There's hardly a thing that he hasn't accused me of—He is the accuser after all. Corrie Ten Boom said, "The first step on the way to victory is to recognize the enemy."[1] Don't skip over that quote too quickly. Read it again.

I don't want to give satan any glory or recognition, but I've fallen prey to his schemes too many times not to know that he is the deceiver and masquerades as an angel of light. However, I'm grateful that I knew the truth and thus recognized that it was the enemy trying to bring me down. And even though I listened to the accusations far too many times than I should have, I also recognized the lie many times and walked in the truth. In fact, many times satan's accusations had the opposite effect on me. They caused me to strengthen my resolve to stand firm on the truth of God's Word and to not give up.

THE ENEMY

The enemy has also tried to hinder me from writing this book. I'll be honest it wasn't easy to make the time to write this book, particularly as I was working a full day and ministering most evenings. However, I wanted to do what God had called me to do and that gave me the edge I needed to push through to start, and then there was no turning back. Even returning to work in the corporate world full time couldn't influence me to abandon this project.

I am a teacher and pastor at heart. As such, it is impossible for me to imagine not sharing what I've learned and experienced in my life. I believe that it is in the spirit of learning and failing and getting up again, that I was able to eventually bring forth this book.

I feel privileged to share my marriage struggles with you and trust that God will transform your life and marriage as you recognize those same lies and struggles in your own life and marriage that you've read in mine.

Here's another BIG truth. Your spouse is NOT your enemy. You are NOT your enemy. The enemy is your enemy. In every battle you need the shield of faith. The Word of God is your shield. Heed the Word of God in your struggle: "This is not a wrestling match against a human opponent. We are wrestling with rulers, authorities, the powers who govern this world of darkness, and spiritual forces that control evil in the heavenly world" (Ephesians 6:12 GW).

The wedding day is easy. Planning the biggest, most important day of your life where you are the star of the show is not only easy; it's super-easy, and it's fun to boot! Anyone can do it. The same cannot be said of the marriage journey. The wedding day is not the end of it. It's only the beginning. There will not be "And they lived happily ever after" unless you commit your marriage to the Lord and allow Him to be the head of your marriage. To be the cord that holds the two of you together. The cord of three strands that is not easily broken (Ecclesiastes 4:12 GNT).

I'm so conscious as I write these words that you may right now be saying to yourself, *It's easy for her to say, she can't even begin to understand what he's done to me and my children.* And you're right. I don't. And I'm not saying you should get divorced or not get divorced. I'm not even saying that dedicating your marriage to God will guarantee a loving marriage for life. What I am saying is that unless God builds your home, you cooperate with Him, and you surrender your will to Him in unity, you are laboring in vain. Allow God to do the work in you.

SHATTERED DREAM

I heard a very sad story of a woman and her shattered dream marriage. She'd been a Christian all her life and grown up in a Christian home with Christian parents and siblings. Their lives honored the Lord and the Word. She married a Christian man with the expectation of living as the Proverbs 31 woman to the fullest degree. They had children together and they raised them in the way of the Lord. She loved her husband with all her heart. She respected, honored, revered, esteemed, and praised him.

Many years later, she forgave him when she found out he had an affair and she forgave with the heart of Christ. She even forgave him the second time when she found out he had another affair after promising her that he would never do that again. She even approached the woman involved and offered her grace and forgiveness too. She prayed for him even more and did all the right things.

But one day, he turned on her with his mean, vicious temper (that she finally admitted he'd always had). He put a gun to her head and was going to end her life. She resigned herself to the fact that she'd be with Jesus that night. Nevertheless, she started praying and asking God to help her. While she was praying, and after what seemed like hours of his insane verbal, mental, physical, and emotional abuse, he suddenly put the gun down and the fight went out of him and he left the room.

That night God told her to get out of her marriage or she would lose her life. And she did. She finally obeyed God. She admitted that God had told her before to get out of the marriage, but she did not listen to Him because she believed He was going to change the situation. She knew God could do anything, and she really believed that if she just prayed long enough and was patient enough, it would eventually happen. However, what changed her mind was that God told her He could indeed change the situation, but unless both parties were 100 percent committed to Him, to the marriage, and to one another, it would not work. God will not go against anyone's will.

That revelation from God was her deciding factor to finally leave her marriage of twenty-five years, which she did, albeit with a very sad and shattered heart. She walked out that day with just the clothes on her back and the determination to never get into that situation again.

What would you have advised her to do?

This is an exceptional story (or maybe not) and we might not hear too many of these stories, but we do hear about marital problems all the time. And as women caring for women, we want to say, "Get out of that marriage, he's not worth it." But Christ died for him too, and only God has the right to judge. She listened to God, and her life was saved because she did.

What I want you to get out of this testimony is that you need to hear from God about whether or not to stay in your marriage. I believe I heard from God when I separated from Kevin, but I would not advise anyone else to do the same thing. That's God's job, not mine.

This woman wept bitter, heartbreaking tears over the loss of her beloved marriage. The wasted years that she gave her all. But there is good news. God was with her all the time. He was and still is her comfort and strength. He is her Redeemer and Restorer of broken walls. She's happily married now, and her children are grown and happily married themselves. They obviously learned some tough lessons from that very sad time too; but praise God that He's their Redeemer and Restorer too.

YOUR LEGACY

What legacy are you leaving your children now? Right now? This very moment in time. Your children desperately need you to be in unity with your spouse and not have strife in the home. They need their parents to lead and guide them by example. If you don't get to your children, and get to them as young as possible, with God's love and grace, be warned that someone or something else will!

Do this because you want your home and family to be counted as a "Kingdom Family for Christ." In the words of Reverend Theodore Hesburgh: "The most important thing a father can do for his children is to love their mother."[3]

Husbands and fathers have such an important role to play in our homes, and it's not impossible or God wouldn't have given it to them. They can take courage from Nehemiah 4:14 (GNT):

I saw that the people were worried, so I said to them and to their leaders and officials, "Don't be afraid of our enemies. Remember how great and terrifying the Lord is, and fight for your relatives, your children, your wives, and your homes."

I truly believe that marriages can be changed and become testimonies for the Kingdom, if husbands and wives conscientiously apply the Word of God to their marriages. In addition, they must maintain unwavering faith that they can and will prevail in the end regardless of the difficulties. And at the same time have the discipline and courage to confront the most brutal facts of the current reality, whatever that might be. "Now all glory to God who is able, through his mighty power at work within us, to accomplish infinitely more than we might ask or think" (Ephesians 3:20).

GOD-ORDAINED GIFTS

Shortly before I started writing this book, my sister Bev, who lives in Perth, sent me an online writing course as a gift. This course was to become the conduit God would use to get my book started. I was so delighted to receive it and I knew it was a God-ordained gift.

I began the course almost immediately and you now hold in your hand the finished product. The course was incredibly helpful, practical, and easy to follow. I will be forever grateful that my sister decided to buy that gift for me. It was just what I needed to start writing this book that God had called me to write many years ago. The course consists of ten modules, and the second assignment was to write a testimonial to myself. I had to write it as if it was written from someone else to me, about the impact the book had on my life.

Finally, I end this book with a testimony that God will do for you what He did for Kevin and me in changing our hearts and transforming our marriage.

Dear Leonie,

I had to write and tell you how much your book has changed my life and marriage! I was also On Divorce Row for so many years, just waiting for the right time to leave. Like you, I felt trapped in a marriage that I felt was love-less and not worth fighting for.

As a Christian woman with a heart for marriage and family, I just could not bring myself to go through with the divorce. In one of the chapters, you wrote that deep in your soul you knew God didn't want you to go through with a divorce, and you quoted Malachi 2:16, where God says that He hates divorce. I could totally relate to that chapter, as I felt the same way and knew that God didn't want me to get divorced either.

However, it never stopped the way I felt about my marriage or my longing for my husband's heart to change and to love me as Christ loves the church, sacrificially as His bride. But as much as I prayed, fasted, sought counseling, tolerated bad behavior, and sought God for the answer to my prayers, things just never seemed to change. But praise God for your obedience in writing this oh-so-honest and much needed book!

Leonie, you have given me practical hope, which I've already put into practice and can you believe it, there has already been a change in my heart and also in my husband. Since I read of how you surrendered everything to God and committed not to ask for any changes in your husband, but to love him as he was, God has honored my commitment too. And I'm trusting that God will raise us up to bring glory and honor to His name and of course to testify of His grace in our marriage and in our lives, which we intend passing on to others.

I'm going to buy a number of copies of your book to give away as gifts and pray over them that God would bless each and every marriage and family for His Kingdom and glory!

From a very grateful sister in Christ,
Nadine

"But God" Chapter 23

I decided to dedicate this final "But God" summary to testimonies from people and ministries that exist to minister to marriages and families.

The following is an extract from: *Biblical Families: The Only Hope for Restoring Society* by Angus Buchan, farmer, author, and international evangelist who lives in South Africa.

Wounded Homes

The most difficult place to be a Christian is at home. This is the area in society that is taking the biggest hit at the moment: families, dysfunctional families, divorced families, families full of abuse. It is so disheartening to read the newspaper, to turn on the TV and to hear the news consistently talking about incest and rape within families. We need to intercede in prayer about the situation at home. The only way that it will be rectified is if we get back to the Word of God. The Bible is very clear about how we should approach this wounded home situation.

A Biblical Design

In Ephesians 5:31, we are reminded that it is "For this reason that a man shall leave his father and mother and be joined to his wife, and the two shall become one flesh." There is too much interference in young marriages by parents. We need to understand that they have to work out their own differences and we need to pray for them.

We need to be there for counsel if they need it and only if they ask for it. We also need to discipline our children; the word of God says if you spare the rod, you will spoil the child and how often have I seen that today. We need to love our children enough to discipline them appropriately.

God's Plan for Marriages

We need to get back to basics. Divorce is not something to take lightly. If you are reading this article and you are already divorced, you need to repent, set things straight and move on. You do not need to live under a cloud of condemnation. Remember the Lord does not condemn His children, He convicts.

The shortcut is not the quickest way home and to make a hasty decision like divorce is not the way out. We need to work through our issues, talk to each other, seek God, ask for forgiveness and press on. We cannot force our wives to submit, we cannot force husbands to love their wives, we cannot force anything in marriage.

The Lord Jesus Christ is our Mediator. He is our go-between and the Bible is the manual for successful marriage. We have to get back to godly Christian marriages in order to show the world the way in which God wants us to live.

Make 'Home' a Priority

We need to put our home situation before anything else. It needs to be before our work, before our sport and even before our ministry. God bless you as you continue to hold the fort.

~

The following poem was written by Jennifer Abbas in 1990, then an eighteen-year-old child of divorce. It can be found in her book, *Generation Ex: Adult Children of Divorce and the Healing of Our Pain.*

Divorce I
The Eruption

Divorce
is like a trembling earthquake
The world shakes
rumbling with rage
and all the anger
guilt
and frustrations
that have been festering for so long
below the surface

suddenly spew upward
in an inferno of haze
widening the gaps
at times
the earth calms
and you think
the turmoil is over
settled
stable
then the cycle begins again
repeating
repeating
repeating.
You are weary
you want to rest
and that is when you realize
the shaking has stopped
but there is an eerie feeling
lurking in the air
you are hesitant to believe
anything
anymore
But you are so tired
after struggling for so long
you rest
on one last solid patch of land
only to watch it crumble in two
two
separate
distinct
parts
that will never come together again
each new patch
supports part of you
and as you watch
they pull away.*

(Dennis and Barbara Rainey are cofounders of Family Life Today and this poem was featured in one of his online family devotionals. Dennis wrote that this is the type of poem that breaks his heart because it represents so many children who are torn apart by divorce. No matter what you are experiencing in your marriage, and no matter how tough it is, just remember the impact that *staying together* will have on your children.)

*Jen Abbas.com Official Site; http://www.jenabbas.com/contribute/ poetry.shtml; accessed October 27, 2017.

~

Ten Ways to Help a Friend's Struggling Marriage
Mitch Temple*

Do you wonder how you can help friends and family members who are struggling in marriage? Here are some time-tested tips and resources to move them away from divorce court and toward reconciliation.

1. Pray for them by name. Ask God to intervene in their marriage. Ask God to give you and others wisdom to know how to help. Pray in their presence as well as when alone. Send emails and note cards of encouragement.

2. Listen. Listening doesn't mean simply hearing. It involves empathizing, seeking to understand and expressing genuine interest.

3. Don't give advice. Your main job is listening. Leave the advice giving to a pastor, counsellor or mentor.

4. Don't make the problem worse. Don't allow your support to be seen as an encouragement to give up or get a divorce. Your job is to help steer them toward the proper help and reconciliation (If addiction or abuse is involved, make sure they get the professional help they need and are safe).

5. Help them think outside the divorce box. Booklets such as *When Your Marriage Needs Help, Should I Get a Divorce,*

and *Marriage and Conflict* can give couples both research and practical advice to help them consider the facts about divorce and how to get the help they need for their marriage.

6. Help them find the right help. Locate a good, licensed Christian counsellor in their area. Ask your pastor or Christian M.D. for a referral. Focus on the Family offers a free counselling consult as well as a free referral service to a Focus-screened marriage therapist.

7. Connect them with a mentor couple. If you are not qualified to help, call your pastor to recommend an older couple who is willing to mentor a younger couple.

8. Refer them to helpful Web sites. Web sites such as Pure Intimacy and FocusOnTheFamily.com offer hundreds of articles, practical advice and resource recommendations on various marriage issues.

9. Encourage them to work on their problems and not simply expect them to be solved on their own. Focus offers an online Marriage Check-up which measures over 18 major areas of marriage—identifying both strengths and weaknesses. This is a good place for a couple to start in addition to working with a professional counsellor.

10. Refer them to solid Christian-based books and seminars. Visit our Family Store for marriage books, broadcast CDs and resources to strengthen a couple's faith through a difficult time. Key resources like Yes, Your Marriage Can Be Saved, Love and Respect, Love Must Be Tough, First Five Years of Marriage, Help! We are Drifting Apart, Breaking the Cycle of Divorce, Healing the Hurt in Your Marriage and others can provide needed encouragement and direction.

* "Ten Ways to Help a Friend's Struggling Marriage," Mitch Temple, *Focus on the Family*; http://www.focusonthefamily.com/marriage/strengthening-your-marriage/mentoring-101/ten-ways-to-help-a-friend-who-is-struggling-in-their-marriage; accessed October 27, 2017.

My prayer for you and your marriage and family:

Heavenly Father,

I come to You in the name of Jesus and in the power of the Holy Spirit for the dear person reading this book. I pray that You would come and bring Your restoration, healing, and grace to the reader, as no one but You can do. Help this precious friend to remember why he/she loved his/her spouse in the first place and that there is nothing You can't do with two hearts that are committed and submitted to You.

I pray for protection of the children and ask that You would bring hope and encouragement to them so that they will not want to give up on life because of their parent's marital strife.

I pray for wives reading this book, Lord, that they would realize that Your love is enough for them and they are complete in Christ. I pray that they would not hunger after love and value from their husbands, who we know Lord, cannot fully give it to them. I pray for the disappointment in their hearts for putting their hope in the wrong places. Fill their lives with Your promises of love and grace so that everything else will dim in comparison.

I pray for each husband reading this book, Father, that You would be their wisdom and guide. That You would show them that no amount of achievement, money, or status can fill the place of Your love. That they need You more than anything else in their lives to fulfill the role You have called them to as heads of their homes, protectors, and providers, and most of all I pray that they would stand and declare as Joshua did, "As for me and my family, we will serve the Lord"!

I pray that You would raise up friends, prayer intercessors, mentors, and counselors to come alongside this reader during struggles and pain.

I pray for resolved financial situations, Lord. That Your child would look to You as the ultimate Provider, and not put pressure on another to carry the burden that You have promised to bear.

I pray for good health, that the stresses of living under strife and conflict would not have a detrimental effect, but that this reader would see that the strife comes from the works of the enemy and a commitment must be made to restore health and wholeness, through You, for everyone in the family.

I pray for marriages that are currently in adultery, that You would convict the hearts, Father, to stop, repent before You, and repair the marriage, getting back on track with You and one another. I pray for the men and women who are caught in self-destructive web of pornography, drug and substance abuse, alcohol abuse, co-dependency, homosexuality, lesbianism, and other such things that are tearing them apart and causing division and strife in their homes.

I pray for everyone who has turned their back on You, Lord Jesus, and backslidden. Call them back to You and cause them to repent before You and turn from their wicked ways and turn back into Your loving arms.

Come, Holy Spirit, wash this dear reader with the water of Your Word and restore love, grace, mercy, joy, and forgiveness to a longing heart so that the marriage and family can bring honor and glory to You, Lord. I pray that Your kingdom, heavenly Father, will be extended with this marriage and family loving and serving You to a thousand generations!

I pray this prayer in the mighty name above all names, Lord Jesus Christ. Amen.

Journal your thoughts:

_____

_____

_____

_____

_____

_____

_____

_____

_____

_____

_____

_____

_____

_____

Journal your prayer:

_____

_____

_____

_____

_____

_____

_____

_____

_____

_____

_____

_____

_____

_____

_____

_____

_____

ENDNOTES

1. A devoted Christian, Corrie Ten Boom and her family helped many Jews escape the Nazi Holocaust during World War II.

2. South African Theological Seminary; https://www.sats.edu.za/4-14-window-church-has-missed-it-2000-years/; accessed October 27, 2017.

3. "Rooted for Life" blog; https://rootedforlife.wordpress.com/2011/03/18/%E2%80%9Cthe-most-important-thing-a-father-can-do-for-his-children-is-to-love-their-mother%E2%80%9D-rev-theodore-hesburgh/; accessed October 27, 2017.

About the Author

At the outset, Leonie Leo-Brewer states that she has a handful of convictions that cannot be shaken. Included in that list are these truths:

> God is good, Jesus is Lord, the Bible is true, life is short, every day is a gift, people matter more than things, fame is fleeting, this world is not my home, and even hard times are meant for my benefit. And at the core of my faith is an unshakable belief in the sovereignty of God. He's God and I'm not. He is sovereign over all the details of my life, and I can trust Him completely, even when those details seem to be spinning out of control.

Leonie is joyfully married to Kevin; they have two married daughters and four precious grandchildren. They make their home in Johannesburg, South Africa. She and her four siblings were raised by both parents in a loving home. She was saved at the age of 42 at an Alpha Course.

In August 2005, Leonie was sponsored to attend a She Speaks writing and speaking training conference through Proverbs 31 Ministries USA. She holds a She Speaks Graduate certificate and is the Director of Proverbs 31 Ministries Africa. With the practical knowledge obtained at the conference, Leonie takes great delight in speaking at women's conferences and meetings and is extending her audience to married couples and men's groups in the future.

In November 2015, Leonie obtained a Distinction in Ministry and Community Services and the Marriage Officers course through the University of South Africa. Leonie's desire is to continue studying to eventually obtain a degree in Ministry and Family Pastoral Care.

Leonie is a full-time woman of God, a part-time women's Bible study leader, Connect Group leader at church, a pre-marriage, marriage and family mentor, and an author and speaker of God's message. Her passion is to join God in building godly marriages and families!

Leonie's life verse sums up her ministry: "But none of these things move me; nor do I count my life dear to myself, so that I may finish my race with joy, and the ministry which I received from the Lord Jesus, to testify to the Gospel of the grace of God" (Acts 20:24 NKJV).

Leonie would love to hear from you.
Please send your comments about this book to
info@leonieleobrewer.com.
Thank you.

For more information about Leonie Leo-Brewer, visit
www.leonieleobrewer.com.

If you would like to invite Leonie to speak to your group, contact her at:
info@leonieleobrewer.com.

www.ingramcontent.com/pod-product-compliance
Lightning Source LLC
Chambersburg PA
CBHW060012050426
42448CB00012B/2720